BETWEEN LAUGHTER AND LIFE

44 CRACKED TALES

SEEMA SINGHAL

For Harshit and Anishka

My greatest inspiration

Contents

Contents

Contents

Preface

For an introvert like me, saying hello for the first time is as difficult as saying goodbye for the last.

The first hello requires overcoming inhibitions, while the final goodbye pulls you from your comfort zone. It's hard to say which is more challenging, but one thing is certain: both lead to new horizons.

I've always loved reading- whether it was a magazine, comic, classic, or bestseller. Writing, however, was never on my mind. But I've always been good at reasoning and persuading people with my words.

Then again, who knows what the future holds? I was content in my small world at home and the vast world of tiny microbes at my office. No one could have predicted the pandemic, and I never imagined my family commitments would surpass my professional ones. When I took a sabbatical during the middle of COVID pandemic, I feared that a sense of emptiness would soon settle in.

During this time, I wrote a piece of poem to motivate my son- I never imagined I'd publish it or write more. Then, I stumbled upon virtual blogging platforms. Saying that first hello to writing wasn't easy, but I took the plunge. In doing so, surprisingly, I met someone unexpected: 'THE NEW ME.' This version of myself had always been there, but I hadn't realized it. Even after returning to work, I never said goodbye to my newfound passion for writing. And here, I present you my first book.

This book is collection of stories from my life, inspired by my surroundings. I hope you'll find something relatable within these pages, where I greet memories while holding onto precious moments- *Between Laughter and Life.*

Acknowledgements

I am deeply grateful to everyone who has been part of this journey and encouraged me to compile my stories.

To my son, Harshit, and my daughter, Anishka- you fill my life with joy and purpose. You are my greatest motivation, and your love inspires me every day to be the best version of myself.

To my husband, Dr Vinay- thank you for your endless patience, understanding, and support, even through the busiest of days. You've stood by me in every chapter of our lives. Thank you for always being my rock, and for believing in me, even when I doubted myself.

To my parents, who instilled in me the values of hard work, resilience, and kindness—your unwavering love and support have been the foundation of everything I do.

To my brothers and sisters-in-law, who have been both my biggest critics and my source of strength. Your presence, whether near or far, has always given me comfort and encouragement.

To my friends, who have cheered me on through every step of this journey- your companionship, support, and encouragement have enriched my life in ways words cannot express. Thank you for always being there.

About The Author

Seema Bansal Singhal is a doctor with over two decades of expertise in the field of microbiology and infection prevention. Writing found its way into her life when she took a sabbatical to support her children. Since then, she has been sharing her thoughts through blogs, short stories, and poetry. Her writing is a reflection of her life experiences, blending her love for words with her commitment to healing.

Born in Aligarh and raised across various cities in Uttar Pradesh, Seema pursued her medical education at the prestigious VSS Medical College, Burla, Odisha and King George's Medical University, Lucknow, Uttar Pradesh. She now resides in Ludhiana, Punjab. She has worked with several medical institutes and corporate hospitals, each experience enriching her professional journey.

A mother to two affectionate and dynamic children, and a wife to a dedicated intensivist, Seema manages her many roles with grace. In her free time, she enjoys reading, painting, and listening to music. A firm believer of 'age is just a number' and 'it's never too late to learn', Seema continues to learn and explore new quests.

Her world revolves around her family and profession and it reflects in her writing. Seema draws inspiration from everyday world around her, both animate or inanimate. Through this book she aims to spread joy, faith, hope and resilience.

About The Book

"Life happens while you are busy making other plans."

Often, it's the small seemingly insignificant moments that leave the deepest impact. It was one such moment, when a doctor discovered her passion for storytelling.

In this heartfelt collection I have weaved together humorous family anecdotes, introspective tales of self-discovery, and reflection of human nature. Each story offers a glimpse into my journey of life, living at my own pace. Ranging from light-hearted memories of amusing and entertaining stories of innocent childhood to the emotional complexities of parenting and deeper reflections on social prejudice and the human nature, these stories blend universal human experiences with wit, wisdom, and warmth. With 44 self-contained, short-stories, this collection invite readers to pause and appreciate the beauty in everyday life. Perfect for busy readers, it allows for dipping in and out at your leisure, incorporating into your busy schedule. More than just a source of entertainment, these stories offer insight into certain human behaviour and encourage self-reflection, resolution, and acceptance. Step into my world to laugh, reflect, and perhaps gain a fresh perspective on your own life.

CHAPTER ONE

The Signature That Made a Lasting Impression!

My son and I were going through his old albums and greeting cards he had made for us when he was young, reliving each moment. When moments become memories, how precious they all become. It was then that he asked, "Mom which was the first thing I scribbled?" I wish I had dated each one. Of all the scribbles, which one was first? I just can't figure it out.

Was it the scribbles on the wall or in my textbooks? (Yes, I was studying for my MD at the time!). Those walls were left behind as we kept shifting and additions of books got updated. I remember having a lot of scribbles in my old books. Right over the most important texts! To the point where the text couldn't be read anymore. People joked, "Abhi se doctori padhana shuru?" And I replied to each one of them, "What he wants to be will solely be his choice, not mine."

When my son was a little grown-up, he wanted to come along with me to the hospitals on his holidays. And I would oblige him on some 'Lucky Days'. God! How he would dance around the whole morning. After all, who wouldn't enjoy all the attention one gets at mum's workplace from her colleagues and subordinates? Each time he would observe a few new things. You know how keenly kids observe and how quickly they learn and imitate? He was no exception. After a few visits, he was quick to analyze that what his mum does during the whole day is to just scribble a few signatures over a few sheets.

"Oh! Just that! What's a big deal? I can also do that." And I don't need to do any medical degree for that. He must have thought. At that time, he wanted to be a doctor just like his mum as all she did was sign a few sheets.

And he did sign quite a few papers over the next few days. Some rough and waste papers and a few were important too. Luckily, not much harm was done and the damage was repairable each time.

Till he noticed that to get money also you just need to sign a small strip of paper. (Read checkbook). He visited the hospital with us and we happened to withdraw money from the bank on the way back to our home.

He must have liked that checkbook very much or he wanted the first-hand experience of signing those thin strips of paper. Not long before he approached my husband with a signed checkbook to receive some money in return.

It seems he got hold of our checkbook and made sure to withdraw a lot of money as he had inscribed almost every leaflet of it.

As a reflex, he got reprimanded. My teary-eyed boy came running to me. He couldn't understand what his fault was. How could his father scold him for helping him out?

He said, "I wanted a lot of money for you. So, you need not go to your workplace. And can stay with me forever."

I was speechless. At that time, I couldn't have made him comprehend why I work. I just embraced him and kissed his forehead. Kids don't keep anything to their hearts. In no time he too forgot.

Now he is grown up. And when I took a sabbatical to help my kids during the testing time. He was the one who wanted me to join back. For he knows I earn more than 'just' money out of my job. I earn respect, self-confidence, and a sense of worth. We take from society and we give back to society with our services. And this 'giving back' factor gives you that high, that can't be replaced with any kind of monetary gain.

For safety reasons, we destroyed those checks. But that artwork is etched in our hearts forever. Each time we narrate this incident, it brings a smile to our faces but he always becomes reticent.

He now knows the worth of a mere signature. And the responsibilities that come with each.

Today he is pursuing his professional degree (no, not medicine) and soon be signing his projects and reports. I'm sure he is going to use his signature for the best. And with style.

Best for him and society. I wish him the success that his signature becomes an autograph. That day my son, I would ask you to sign my palm, as my heart is already full of your imprints.

CHAPTER TWO

Chin Up, However Your Heart Breaks

I always felt protected between those two pairs of arms. They were my world. Wherever I went, I felt safe within those strong arms, protecting me like a fortress. My parents. I believed that it would be like this forever. My parents and I- that was my small world.

I felt insecure whenever another kid approached one of my parents especially my mother. I would retreat into silence unable to express my feelings. I would be reclusive and it would take a lot of courage to come out of that shell and come to terms with my mother's err. How could she adore a child who wasn't me? Eventually, I would forgive my mother but not that child. I would make sure that I never became friends with that child.

It was time to spread wings and explore the world, my parents declared. But I was happy the way it was; I had no intention of exploring. Especially, if it required to come out of the secure fortress of my parents' arms. But my parents were adamant that I join a school. Finally, after discussing the topic numerous times among themselves, it was the day when I accompanied them to visit that school. I kind of liked it but not at the cost of leaving behind my refuge. I didn't have that much courage.

That day Mumma accompanied me and stayed with me. I played with other kids by stealing frequent glances at my mother. She stayed with me as she promised and brought me back with her.

The next day, I was supposed to stay there for a longer period. As my mother dropped me at school and was about to leave, I was scared and wailed. I ran behind her but two strong arms held me from behind and that day I felt like strong arms may not be protective always. Those arms that kept me separated from my mother. She said she would be back within an hour, but it seemed like forever. I didn't feel like playing that day. I waited for her and she returned to pick me up after what felt like an eternity to me.

In the coming days, I tried to gather some courage and I found some. Soon, I was acquainted with everyone at school and didn't fear anyone. It felt like fluttering my wings a little. I grew to love it but always looked forward to returning to the security of my home.

Time flies when you are comfortable. Then it was that time when I needed to change school.

"What is wrong with this one?" I asked.

"You have outgrown this one." They replied.

I felt they were exaggerating. No one paid heed to my opinion and made me go to the new school. I was afraid, though I didn't cry this time. I think I was courageous.

Later, I attended a few more schools and colleges. Each time it took some courage. But I managed to adjust.

I learned to flutter and flap my wings and to stay afloat.

I made my nest and I have my family now. Protecting my nestlings requires the courage to give them the freedom to explore the world. And mom, pa, I feel you when I remember my first day at school.

As I dropped my little angel off at his school, I realized it took much more courage than I had anticipated.

Letting go of your little one takes a lot of courage. Whether it is first day of school or the college. It's a time in my life when I need to overcome my fears and have the courage to let my older child to explore the world on his own. It seems tough but when I reflect on my own experiences, it both gives me courage and makes me ponder the emotions my parents must have felt at that time.

CHAPTER THREE

When Smiles Hide Tears

It is not that I have never seen his sensitive or weak side but still, he chose to hide those few emotions and I couldn't understand him. I even complained to my mother on a few occasions and neither of my parents tried to come clean on that.

Since my childhood, I heard my father saying that he would get me married only in a nearby city so whenever he would want to meet, he could reach me within an hour or two. But I was destined to go for studies at a place where it took thirty hours or so to reach, and that too at the age of eighteen years and not for a year or two but for six long years.

He accompanied me to my admission formalities at the medical college and never looked back after dropping me there. I cried like a child when his train's departure time passed, and he hadn't turned up to say goodbye!

Each time after vacation, when I would leave to go back to my hostel, he would come with me to see me off at the station. As soon as I boarded the train, he would say, "You carry on with your friends. The train will leave in a few minutes; I'm getting late for the office." He would leave assuring me, without waiting for the train's departure. My heart cried silently, wondering why he couldn't wait for a few more minutes, till the train started chugging away? I wanted to see him and wave my hand till I could no longer make out his tall frame.

This continued for a couple of years till one day I saw him standing in a corner on the station watching me from a distance and dabbing his eyes. The moment our eyes met, I shouted PaPa......and then train started chugging. I couldn't get the chance to speak to him. He just waved his hand with a big smile before turning around but I sensed the struggle behind that smile.

This was about thirty years back and those were days when getting connected on phone calls was a luxury and anyways, I couldn't have called him until I had reached my destination and that was going to take more than a day.

I can't express my emotions in words and about what I went through the whole day. I was sad, upset with myself, and incredibly homesick. I wanted to fly back and hug him. I wanted to confess what I had thought about him all those years. I wanted him to know that it doesn't matter at all if he showed his softer side to his offspring as he would still be the same most dependable person I know.

By the time I reached my destination, I had cried my heart out and was calm and none of us talked about it, out of respect for each other's sentiments. I understood that he just wanted me to remember his smiling and happy face as I was the one going far away. He didn't want to further weaken my already vulnerable spirits, so he always hid that pang behind his smiles.

But that day his smile said it all.

CHAPTER FOUR

Connect for Happiness

The other day, I was playing *Connect Four* with my daughter.

As you know, it's a two-player board game; though one can play it on a computer as well, I prefer board for obvious reasons. The board is made up of horizontal and vertical columns that contain slots, and players alternate their turn dropping one of the discs into an unfilled column until one of them achieves four in a row either horizontally, vertically, or diagonally and wins the game.

You can play defensively by thwarting the other player or offensively by focusing on connecting four in a row first.

I was playing defensively, focusing only on blocking her discs from connecting, while she was simply focusing on making her four connect. That difference in our attitudes decided who won the game that day.

When we were midway through filling the board, my daughter exclaimed, "Mumma! you missed noticing that you won the game on your last move. I didn't see it either. I'm sorry!"

"Rules are simple; since I didn't claim victory, I lost my chance to win. Keep on dropping your disc." I asserted.

But she wasn't ready to let go of my win and was genuinely concerned about how I could have missed it. As 'The Mumma' whose eyes capture everything, including what is happening behind her back, she asked, "Mumma, I was busy making my four connect, but how could you miss it when you accomplished the task?"

The answer was hidden in her question. I replied, "because I was so obsessed with blocking your disc from connecting, I missed noticing mine."

Isn't it true that while we are busy ridiculing others' triumphs, we forget to celebrate our little moments? We are so busy lingering over our past that we forget to dwell in the present. We let negative people affect us and create a wall that prevents positivity from reaching us. We compare our real life with others' perfect virtual lives and ruin our own substantial moments. We hold on to past grudges and keep on blaming others for the lack of self-happiness.

Rather, we should remember to declutter our minds, forgive, let go of the past, practice gratitude, allow positivity to break through that barricade of negativity, and surround ourselves with positive people who encourage us. By being benevolent, you can fill your heart with contentment and happiness. It's always a two-way process; you spread happiness to receive it back in abundance.

I promise to remember the principle of happiness. Do you?

CHAPTER FIVE

Am I a Cool Mom?

It was year 2021. Covid was at its peak, and all the school and colleges were shut, leaving the kids on their own with only virtual classes and guidance. The use of gadgets was also at its peak. It was testing time for those students who were appearing for boards and entrance exams. My son was one of them.

My son was busy with his practice test for the next entrance exam which was going to be conducted next week. We were waiting for the release of answer keys for the one he had already appeared.

"The answer key has just been released. Calculate his score and let me know." My husband texted me to calculate his score on the last exam that he had appeared last week.

I checked and calculated. He hadn't scored as well as we had expected (or rather, as we wanted. I hate to confess, but the result was exactly what he had attempted and shared with us).

"Your 'X' friend has scored more than 99th percentiles. You haven't been able to improve your percentile that much. You can discuss if you need some help." I tried to be as cool as I could. After all, I'm coming of age, cool mom.

I knew I should not have compared two children. I also knew, I shouldn't push him beyond his potential, and I assure you, I was not doing any of that. I was 'just' asking.

My son could have acted two ways after looking at his scoresheet.

Either he could be depressed or cool.

If he was depressed, I would have worried. "Don't be saddened beta, just forget this and think about the next exam. Are you better prepared as compared to last week?" Though I knew the answer myself, still I wouldn't have hesitated to probe him.

But I got a look from him for an answer.

He was calm, my tension increased exponentially. "How come you can perform better if you never take any tension? Thoda tension jaruri hai beta."

I got another look while he tried his best to look worried. Whether to please me or to save himself, I would never know.

I think I'm a cool mom, still, he doesn't share his true feelings with me. (Because, when he shares, I seldom believe him.) Are you hiding something? You know, it's a mother's birthright to doubt everything.

I wasn't pushing him to the edge, just asking. I told you na, I'm a cool mom.

"You have already secured a seat in one of the best colleges. I'm very happy about it. But you know that place is so far away and its pandemic. I'm worried about you. It will be good for all of us if you can get a college near to our place." I reminded my son simultaneously adding, "You don't need to stress, just keep trying a little more."

You know I'm a cool mom.

Though my son had done fairly well in his competitive exams, like any typical parents, our expectations increased a bit each time he achieved a new level. We pushed him a little more. We set another target for him, added more stress on ourselves and put even more pressure on him.

What if he had gone to a moderately good college instead of the best one? I know many people around me who are doing fairly well in their life and no one asks them which college they attended. I also know a few who were considered the cream of the lot and finally have performed moderately in life. Then it's as per my judgment. Their success is good till they are fine with it.

Definition of success is subjective just like the definition of happiness. What gives me happiness is not necessarily true for different lots. How I define success might not fit in the definition of other people.

So, should we have left him (my son) on his own?

What if he had asked later, why didn't you push me a little more? This was my dilemma!

I have seen and met some of them, who asked this question later.

There is a very thin line between right and wrong and between guiding and forcing.

I knew it was a crucial time for him. I should have thought about his wellbeing instead of boosting my ego. I should not have worried as he had already done fairly good instead, I should have told him the pros and cons of the options he would get in each circumstance and then left it to him.

After all, it's his life and he should be allowed to choose his battles. Either he will cherish the victory or would learn the lesson, but definitely he would win the battle.

CHAPTER SIX

Am I a Mean Mom? It's OK... Let's Infuse Some Gratitude

The same year, it was my daughter's birthday week and for her, birthday celebration meant friends, party, food, cake and gifts and why shouldn't it be? After all, she was as demanding and as normal as any kid of her age could be.

But that year she was not as excited as she used to be, because of the restricted atmosphere. It was clear to her that party was going to be just family affair and gifts and cake she could have of her choice.

Now, she was trying to grab as many toys as possible, and I gave in to her request because, like a normal, emotional parents, we wanted to provide our kids with what we couldn't have.

She got her first gift, and within 48 hours was already regretting accepting that life-size soft toy, which had cost me a fortune, and she wanted the other one she had seen on the shelf in that toy shop (she chose it herself weighing it over many other toys at the toy shop).

It was hard on me, thinking, why am I not able to make her happy?

Am I not doing enough for her?

I searched and read about child psychology and such behavior, and this made me realize that I needed to put more effort into teaching her about gratitude.

Kids should be taught to feel gratitude and appreciate the hard work we put in to raise them and provide for their needs. I found that gratitude makes one happier. It helps to improve our overall well-being because gratitude is proven to improve physical as well as mental wellbeing.

Grateful kids are less materialistic, less self-centered and more optimistic.

Gratitude helps kids to stay resilient in hard times.

Being grateful reduces jealousy and the need to have "more".

Let's see the ways how I incorporated it in real life.

1. If you are a complainer, cut back on it and focus on reframing every negative situation.

Kids absorb everything they see and hear. I often hear my kids repeat words they've picked up from adults or peers, even if they have heard them only once.

Instead of complaining about the traffic, you can use the time to have fun or talk with your family. I play *"stone, paper, scissor"* while waiting for the green signal at the traffic light. And believe me, my daughter prays to get a red signal at every crossing. Phew!

2. Rule that helps me decide

I do not buy them anything that does not fit in their room (or in our house).

If they want a toy, but their room is full, I say NO.

Now, if they have toys that they no longer play with, I encourage them to buy the new one when they give away the old ones to less fortunate people.

3. Experiences are important rather than stuff

The pleasure in getting something you want, no matter how expensive it is, stays with you for a few days. After that, you get used to it and no longer cherish it.

But experiences are memories etched in your heart. Experiences have the power to make you happy even after many years. Rather than collecting things, focus on giving children more experiences.

4. Have a daily gratitude routine

If you want to make your kids grateful, having a gratitude routine helps a ton.

You can set a time in your day to do this. We do it usually before bedtime. Before putting them to sleep, I ask them to say two or three good things that happened that day for which they are grateful.

If they have nothing to say, I prompt them by asking, "Are you grateful that you have a loving family?", and that's a yes.

On any given day, we have lots of blessings to be thankful for. This practice helps kids (and us) stay in gratitude consistently.

Some lessons are hard to teach, then you need to do it someday anyway.

A Balancing Act

"It doesn't need much care. Just keep it in direct sunlight and water it only when the upper soil is dry." the nursery person briefed me on the care of the Bougainvillea sapling before handing it over to me. I was in the process of upgrading my so-called garden. In the absence of the required proper place to develop a kitchen garden, I fulfill my wish to have one by keeping multiple planters with a variety of plants. I keep on adding a few each month which gives me a sense of contentment and happiness.

That day, I bought two varieties of Bougainvillea- one the usual pink and the other pure white. For some reason, white flowers attract me a little more than colorful ones.

I love Jasmine for its fragrance, Plumeria for that central yellow shade and its overall beautiful pattern, and Bougainvillea for its bountiful bloom. It always blooms in big bunches and retains its beauty even after the flowers have withered.

Returning to that day, I planted those saplings in my garden and started waiting for the bouquet. I care a lot for my plants, watering, pruning or plucking old leaves from the branches. I need to attend to my plants at least twice a day. But somehow, I forgot the advice from the gardener. I watered it regularly. It thrived but didn't flower.

I couldn't understand the reason. The plant was healthy with the greenest leaves. I again went to the nursery to ask for some advice. The gardener suggested I keep it out of my sight. No need to look at it daily. Just forget about it. Have a look after a week.

I shifted it on the terrace, and after a week I saw small buds! One more week and the plants were full of flowers. I was so happy. The most beautiful magenta and white flowers.

Sometimes in our enthusiasm, we care too much and it only harms us. The plant was getting enough water, so it ceased focusing on survival. The moment conditions became a little harsh, it started to flower to protect itself and produce its progeny. Same goes for our children. The more comfort we provide to our kids, the less they learn to fight. Balance is the key. Nurture them, but let them spread their wings. So, when the time comes, they are ready to take that flight and soar high.

CHAPTER EIGHT

Yes, I am Guilty of Setting the Wrong Example

She saw him entering the house and sprinted towards her kitchen.

Her kitchen. A small box comprising of a plastic gas stove, cookware, and a little, cute tea and snacks set.

Instantly, she began organizing everything and started preparing tea. She emulated pouring some water into the pan. Switched on the gas stove. Put some ginger, sugar, and tea leaves. Let it boil. Added some milk and let it simmer for some time before straining into a cup. Just the way he likes it. She remembers every step perfectly.

Simultaneously, she put a slice of bread in her toy toaster. Then she served it on a plate. A small white plastic dish with a flowery sticker in the center.

By the time I fetched tea and snacks for my husband she was already standing in front of him with a tray. A tray containing an empty cup in a saucer and a plate with plastic butter toast.

He, her father, and my husband had just returned from work. Very tired and not in a mood to play kitchen-kitchen with her.

But did he have any option? No. He didn't have the heart to break her heart. So, he first picked up a cup from her tray and mimicked taking a large sip from it. Hoping the game gets over soon.

"Papa, slowly. It's scalding hot. You will get your tongue seared." she stopped him midway.

I sat beside him and gave him a meaningful smile. *"You can't get away with it quickly and so easily. She has trapped you; you have to play with her now."*

"Papa, take a bite from this toast as well. This is very tasty. You must be very hungry."

He pretends to take a bite from it, then asks for her permission to take a sip of the actual tea as well, which she gracefully grants.

She is our daughter, only four years old at that time, maybe even younger. I don't exactly remember.

This was one of her first kitchen tales.

We smiled and played along with her. We went all gaga over her good observation skills.

I don't lead her to play 'the kitchen'. Neither do I prevent my son. But my son never asked for one. No one had ever gifted him a kitchen set or a dollhouse. But at the age of four, my daughter had three kitchen sets and two dollhouses.

I didn't require to instruct her that kitchen work was her duty and not her brother's. Nevertheless, somehow, she got it that way. Though, I intended to teach cooking skills to both my kids. At the right time. But they both must have already formed an opinion about whose duty it was.

She was doing what she observed.

Kids ideate parents and perceive their surroundings.

We all need to set an example very carefully.

CHAPTER NINE

I Promise the Moon

Child: "Mom, where is the moon today? You know, I get scared when nights are so dark."

Mother: "Today it's a new moon night. Look at the sky! There are so many stars gleaming brightly."

Child: "But mom! What's the use of so many stars if they can't chase away the darkness? They might look bright in themselves, but they still cannot illuminate the world."

Mother: "It's not like that honey. They glow day and night, but they seem to serve no other purpose than being bright beautiful celestial bodies in the faraway sky. They are so far away that their brightness doesn't reach here but some are even bigger and hotter than our Sun. Yet, they appear as minuscule dots in the sky.

Though present throughout the day, you can only notice them when night falls. It gives us a lesson that just because something or someone seems invisible doesn't mean that they are so. You should keep on doing your bits without worrying about getting recognized.

Someone struck by Cupid might glance at them, or a curious star-gazer might spend an evening admiring their beauty. And for someone who has lost a loved one, they may look to the stars, finding hope or a connection to their beloved who have otherwise gone so far.

Look at that moon - it appears and disappears as it pleases. It doesn't even shine with its own light but reflects the Sun's beam. Like a perfect teammate, it brightens the night when the Sun goes down to light the other half of the world. It teaching us the value of teamwork.

It stays in the sky, doing its small bit to brighten the night for the otherwise dark world.

Lovers swear by its beauty, the epitome of love, even though it shines with borrowed light. Still, it does its bit to make the night less dark.

Then don't we all need a break from our monotonous life? So, I think even the moon has all the right to take a break once in a while."

Child: "But Mumma! don't you need a break?"

Mother: "I do, but my life revolves around you, my dear. You are my world, and I am your Moon."

Child: "And Papa?"

Mother: "He is our shining star, The Sun, who brightens our days. Whenever he goes down, Mumma, the Moon steps in for him. Don't worry as long as we're here, we will make sure your nights are as bright as your days."

Tommy

Betrayed And Lost

He was born to a stray dog, in the backyard of a kind family. God only knows what compelled my brother to pick this light brown pup from the whole litter even before he opened his eyes. My brother must have been only in his teens. He brought him home, hiding in the pocket of his pajamas, afraid to face our parents. He was afraid because he didn't ask for their permission before adopting a pup but he didn't have the heart to abandon him either. The calling had come from inside.

A meeting was called by him and all four of us gathered on the porch of our house. Who will and how to present the case to the mother, and how? We couldn't think of a convincing solution. I don't remember who disclosed the situation to Mumma but the verdict on the case was exactly what we had anticipated.

"Go and return him where he belongs." But she gave some milk to feed him first.

Both of my elder brothers took him with them and roamed around the street, racking their brains hard for a solution, and soon they found one. They came back home, the pup still in their hands, "His mother is not accepting him back."

"How do you know? Just leave him with her and he shall be fine." My mother asserted.

"We did leave him with her but she didn't allow him to feed. We observed from a distance the whole time. We thought he would starve to death, so, we brought him back," they lied, trying to emotionally manipulate her. And it worked perfectly. They had successfully pressed her weakest nerve. We saw our mother's eyes soften.

And yeah! Permission granted. He was allowed to stay, but with few conditions. My brothers promised to attend to all his needs and requirements. Already having enough on her plate, my mother refused to take responsibility for him, except for cooking for him as well.

You know promises are made to be broken. And they did break this promise too. Gradually, all his responsibilities shifted to my mother, though even she didn't realize it. But she never complained either.

He was called Tommy. This is how Tommy became one of the members of our family.

Only a few months had passed since he had come to our house. Everyone was happy with this new inclusion in our family except my father. He didn't approve of him but no one seemed to care about his opinion on this matter.

One day, at mealtime, I decided to feed him with my hands. As I offered him bread, a piece fell from my hand.

As soon as I tried to pick up that piece, he pounced, and before I could withdraw my hand, he was swinging from it, his teeth pierced deep into my flesh.

It happened right in front of my father. He was angered beyond limits to see the condition of my hand. Although Tommy seemed to feel guilty, he wasn't forgiven for this. The same day, he was kicked out to the outskirts of the city. My father took him and my brother for a ride and left Tommy there.

With his exit, he took away all the peace and joy. All of us were miserable. There was a cold war-like situation at my house. No one was complaining to anyone. No one was blaming anyone. At least not directly. But everyone had something to say and the eyes conveyed this to each other.

It was my mistake, the way I behaved. I shouldn't have interfered with his meal. And abandoning the poor guy was too harsh a punishment on the part of my father.

Within few hours of my father leaving him there, my brothers went back in search of him, but they couldn't find him. Not that day... not next day... and not the day after that...

Everyone was quiet and hurt. All of us felt like we had betrayed a speechless animal. My mother felt sad thinking that street dogs wouldn't let him survive since a pet wouldn't have that strong survival instinct they have. We would talk about him the whole day but fall silent as soon as my father entered the house.

Father could sense that life was not returning to normal, even though three days had passed. He also knew that my brothers were searching for him every day. He must have been feeling guilty too but wouldn't admit it. He actually hadn't comprehended, before taking that drastic step, that everyone, including my mother, had become so attached to Tommy in such a short span.

But the damage had been done, perhaps beyond repair. Or was there more to unfold? Who knew?

Found And Contented

A poor soul was betrayed, abandoned, and left to himself after being provided with a comfortable life for a few months. Had we not adopted him, he would have been tough and adapted to the street life. This thought was killing all of us. We had lost all hopes of getting him back and prayed for his safety every day.

They say, that a dog never forgets its way back. Had he wandered to the place, he would have returned by now. But he had been ridden on a two-wheeler, so the chances were slim that he would be able to find the way back to us. The second reason, which we dreaded to even think of, could have been that he was chased by some wild stray dogs and was hurt. We were trying to make peace with the fact that he wasn't with us anymore.

A few days had been passed. We all were in deep slumber that night when my mother heard some noises at the main gate. She focused on listening more, and we all too got up. Sure, someone was whining and whimpering and it could not be anyone other than Tommy. Suddenly we all felt an adrenaline rush.

The time was three in the morning. As we opened the door, there he was standing tall on his hind legs, trying to reach and climb the gate. Now, wagging his tail and as soon as the gate was opened, he rushed in, jumped on us, and licked all of us. He was covered in mud, infested with ticks, and had scratches over his body.

Immediately, he was taken inside. He looked so week, hurt and hungry. After giving him some water and food he was made to sleep. In the morning, after a thorough cleaning and full body examination, we tended to the bruises and ticks he had gotten in those days.

This time my father didn't say anything. Though he must have heard all the ruckus early in the morning, he didn't get up at that time. Tommy was playful around him, holding no grudges against anyone. He simply forgave everyone.

He must have remained in hiding during the daytime and walked through the night. It took him a few days to find his way back but he did find the path. This time straight to our hearts. Whatever we did to him he didn't lose trust that he would be welcomed back. We were so glad that he showed that trust and returned to us.

Within a few days, he was again the same naughty and exuberant pup he was used to be. Soon, he grew into an adult. He was a terror for the others but reality was a bit different. His barks were worse than his bite, literally. He was loving towards most of the neighbors, except a few who made the mistake of teasing him once. Their scent from a far distance was sufficient to make him mad. If it were up to him, he would have changed their path. However, they tried to make peace with him, but alas! He remained enemies with them for his whole life. He would invariably growl and charge at those few people.

If barks could kill, he would have killed all the strangers. But only from the distance. The moment, someone came near to the gate, he would run inside on the pretext of calling mother. She would then take charge of the situation. While he would continue to support her from behind. In the literal sense. His hind legs behind and front body beside her and barking endlessly until he got scolded by mother.

There are so many memories of him. He was like the youngest kid of the home, cute and pampered.

Tommy stayed with us for seven years. Later he suffered some health issues and left this world in the arms of my brother, the one who adopted him first.

CHAPTER ELEVEN

I Saw Them Dancing

It must have been 3 AM. I couldn't recall why, but my sleep was interrupted. It was dark inside the room, but I could make out the silhouette of everything. It must have been moonlight.

Well, I didn't get up or try to turn my gaze, but whatever came into my field of vision, I was able to appreciate. My younger brother was sleeping beside me. On another bed, my brother and my father were sleeping. My mother was sleeping behind me on a charpoy but I dared not look back in that direction. How could I? Beyond her bed was that window, and outside that window was that forbidden Peeple tree.

I turned further towards my brother and hugged him. I closed my eyes. I wanted to get back to sleep, as the room was already starting to feel eerie. The moment I closed my eyes, I noticed something on the wall. Terrified, I opened my eyes to confirm. My worst fear had come alive.

The ghosts were dancing on the wall. I could hear the music as well. *"Scary creatures dance to the tune of scary music,"* I thought to myself. The last time my grandmother visited us, she told us stories of ghosts. They dwell on the Peepal trees. One was right outside our room's window. "Never go near the Peepal tree at night. Ghosts live on Peepal trees. They sleep during the day but dance through the night."

"I won't sleep tonight. I'll sit by the window. I want to watch them dancing." I declared dreamily. "If you watch them dancing, they take you along with them, and soon you become one of them," she explained and I believed her.

Though mistakenly, now I had seen them dancing. "*Soon, I'm going to be one of them. maybe I should close my eyes and they would never know I have seen them dancing.*" I shut my eyes tight.

But my bladder betrayed me just at the wrong time. I needed to pee urgently. "*What could I do now? If I get up, they are going to know about me.*" I thought to myself. The urge was too intense.

"Mummmmma... mummmmmma..." I stammered without turning towards her, as quietly as I could. Just for my mother's ears. I couldn't take any risks. It seemed she was in deep sleep.

I tried again, "Mummmmmmma... Mummmmmmma..." a little louder this time, hoping it would rouse her from her sweet slumber.

My worst fear came alive. I saw a bigger shadow on the wall. It looked like a 'she' ghost. I could make out her long hair as it tried to smooth her braid before coming in through the window. She started moving toward me. The shadow was getting larger as she came nearer.

I forgot about needing to pee. "Maybe I can still befool her." I shut my eyes tightly and held my breath too.

After a few moments, I tried to peek from the corner of my eye. The ghost was going back out from the window. I sighed with relief and went back to sleep. I must have slept after that, because the next thing I knew, it was morning, and my dear mom was waking me up.

"You woke me up in the night and then slept yourself," she asked me, smiling.

"Shhh...Shhh... don't talk about it, I fooled them, but they might still hear," I confided in her.

Mumma shrugged, unable to understand. "This girl and her tales," she muttered, and I ran to the washroom to empty my bladder.

I was about four years old at the time. Usually, you don't remember much from that age, but this, I remember as if it happened yesterday. This is one of a few early memories I have. What I have described above were my feelings at that time, what I went through.

You must have understood by now that I saw shadows of the tree and leaves and heard the rustling of leaves and chirping of crickets. Another shadow was of my mother which I misunderstood as a ghost's shadow. Years later, as I grew up, it became clear to me. But that night was the scariest night of my life. I didn't pee that night and I didn't share the story with anybody. We don't realize it, but sometimes these stories leave an everlasting impression on young minds.

CHAPTER TWELVE

My Riding Fiasco

"She is not to ride a two-wheeler; she is born to drive a four-wheeler." This was not a forecast from a saint but a satire on my inability to learn to ride a bicycle.

Being the only girl among four siblings, I was always overprotected. Eventually, I was turned into a delicate darling who was always afraid of getting hurt. From 9th standard onwards, I was supposed to manage my school transportation myself. However, I was still waiting for the right time to learn how to ride a bicycle. Although I did not mind walking to school, my father wanted me to use a bicycle.

Soon, my father bought a bicycle, keeping in mind everyone's requirement. The size suited my eldest brother but it lacked the bar that was typically part of male bicycles in those days, so I could ride it easily. My brothers' schools were within walking distance, so they only needed a bicycle for fun rides in the evening, while I could use it to go to school. His plea was, "Size doesn't matter. Anyone can ride a bicycle of any size if they know how to ride it. Cycles are just cycles; the mere presence of a bar doesn't define them as men's or women's." Period.

But I, not wanting to take any risks, insisted on riding only one, with a height that allowed my feet to reach the ground when seated. So, whenever I sensed danger, I could put my foot down.

And I did put my foot down. I didn't ride that bicycle, citing that it was way too big for me, and my brothers didn't ride it because they felt embarrassed about riding a woman's bicycle.

Poor father! His vision of hitting two birds with a one stone backfired. Total flop!

My brothers, being mature, clever, and in the majority, came up with a solution. If they could teach me to ride, this one could probably be assigned to me permanently and they would be in the position to demand another one. This time a male version of it. My eldest brother took command. Though our age gap was just four years, he always showed the maturity and wisdom of someone forty years old. My sessions started the next day. He assured me that he wouldn't let me fall or get hurt if I followed all his instructions.

The next day, in the early morning three of us got ready. I was ready to take the lessons, my brother to give them, and my father was the silent spectator. I was made to climb at the seat while my brother held the bicycle and pushed. He asked me to keep pedaling, saying, "Don't worry, I'll run alongside your bike and won't leave you at any point."

As soon as I started pedaling, my handlebars went out of control. He saved me from falling and reframed his instructions. "Keep pedaling but balance your handlebars as well".

Poor me! either I could focus on the handle or the pedal. So, I resigned, "I can't do both together."

He felt like quitting too but the thought of riding a lady's bicycle must have prevailed a sense inside his head.

With a composed attitude, he tried again, "OK! you balance the handlebar first and try to pedal in between. I'll keep pushing."

Poor guy! He ended up pushing the whole time while I enjoyed a free ride. At the end of the session, as soon as I uttered, "Ah! The weather is so cool today," I got a hard stare from my tired and sweat-soaked brother.

This went on for a day or two until one night, I dreamt of riding a bicycle all by myself like a pro. I got up. It was almost morning and I couldn't sleep after that.

"Do you think morning dreams always come true?" I asked my mother.

"Yes, they say so." My mother replied.

"You just watch, I'm going to learn it today," I announced zealously and determinedly.

That day, I agreed to ride unassisted after the first push. I did it!!! I made it without falling or getting hurt. My whole family cheered me.

The commotion on the road made all of my neighbors come out. A few of them had already witnessed my—or should I say, my brother's—struggle. I still remember that thumbs up from my neighbor. The moment I bowed to acknowledge it, Thadaaaak! Everyone heard. I could not understand what had happened. But in the next moment, I was on the side of the road with my bicycle resting on top of me.

I was all bruised and bleeding and stunned. My sessions ended that day and so did my dream. My mother scolded everyone. I still carry that day's physical scar on my left hand.

The fate of that bicycle? Let's not discuss it!

CHAPTER THIRTEEN

1984: Cricket, Indira, and My India

"Which one is the best cricket team in the world, Papa?" I asked my father.

He was busy preparing something to eat while listening to the cricket commentary on his transistor. The year was 1984. With my mom away at her Mayka due to some unavoidable situation, my father the 'man of the house' was cooking. I had been watching him for some time, alternating between moving the spatula and listening, reacting to the balls being smashed and wickets falling. That raised my curiosity to know better about cricket and the best team. I still wasn't drawn to the game. You could blame it on my young age or limited exposure.

"India," he replied rather proudly.

Did I hear 'India' correctly?

It took me a few seconds to comprehend the information. whenever I reminisce about that moment, I still get goosebumps. I found myself reliving that moment of pride while writing this article. I am one of many who were there when India inscribed history by winning the world cup. Unfortunately, I neither understood and nor witnessed the moment. But I still feel proud that I'm one of that generation. Those who were born before 1983 can understand my emotions very well.

Though India won the world cup again, the first is always more precious. Especially since no one in the world had predicted that India could win world cup back in 1983.

It was also the year when knowledge about the world around me was making some sense to me. Just as I was coming to terms with India's prowess in cricket, I was also growing up in the shadow of another powerful figure: Mrs. Indira Gandhi, our Prime Minister. Being a citizen of a country that had the world's best cricket team and a woman Prime Minister who had served for the long time, I felt proud, not just of my country, but of the sense of security that came from knowing we had a powerful leader. A woman leader.

In my early years, I saw, rather heard Mrs. Indira Gandhi ruling our country with elan. She was the most powerful woman I knew during my childhood. The woman who wouldn't let me believe in the stories of the unfortunate state of women I heard about in our society. How could women in my country be in a sorry state when a woman had been prime minister for so long? I still don't understand.

I was innocent and naive. I didn't know that situations and ranks could change. In that match, I don't remember exactly who the other team was but India didn't win. I was disheartened.

When news of assassination of our Prime Minister broke later that year, I was struck by a deep sense of vulnerability, as though the ground beneath my feet had shifted. I couldn't have imagined my country without Mrs. Indira Gandhi. I felt vulnerable.

CHAPTER FOURTEEN

Warmth, I Got in Return

"Happiness is not something readymade. It comes from your own actions."- Dalai Lama

I often drove through that red light, and almost every time, I noticed a lady with an infant in her arms and a toddler tugging at her clothes, following her closely. My heart ached to see her begging on the road with two kids. Many times, I thought about starting a conversation with her but couldn't gather the courage. I was a little apprehensive due to an experience I had when I asked a young lad who was begging, if, given an opportunity, would he like to do some work to earn his livelihood?

He gave me a look as if he couldn't comprehend me or as if I were an alien on this earth.

There must have been some reasons for her situation, and she must have been very helpless to be doing that. I was in no position to judge her actions because I wasn't in her shoes. In fact, she didn't even have shoes on her feet. (Pun intended)

Winter was approaching, and one day, I saw her and her kids shivering from the cold. Whatever they were wearing was not enough for the harsh weather.

When I returned home that day, I searched my house for the old clothes and packed a bag for her. Few sweaters, that I wasn't using anymore, and some small clothes that my kids had outgrown. I also packed a few packets of biscuits. I kept that bag in my car.

The next time when I saw her, I gave her the bag, which she gladly accepted. we couldn't exchange words as traffic started moving and people began honking behind me.

The next time I noticed her, she was wearing the same clothes. Although she was quite far from my car, the gratitude and happiness I saw on her face were priceless. So was the happiness in my heart- warmer than any woolen clothes!

It didn't cost me anything, but the happiness and content I received was priceless.

CHAPTER FIFTEEN

Meera's Monsoon Tale

Everyone welcomes the rain after a hot, dusty, and dry season. Even the earth looks new after a few torrential showers on its parched surface.

From hopping in the puddles and floating the paper boats to enjoying the drizzle quietly sitting by the window with a hot cup of tea and fritters, and listening to the music, I had come a long way.

I never liked heavy downpours but loved the drizzles. My reason was simple, no one allowed me to go outside till it slowed down a little. Anyways, once I sneaked out when it was raining heavily and the experience didn't go nicely with me. I never tried again after that.

The reasons elders disliked heavy downpours were different, and I didn't understand them at that time. Difficulty in commuting to workplace, piles of laundry waiting to see sunlight, and we kid ready to add one more round to this. I understood it only when my karma paid me back.

A few years back, on one such monsoon day, it was pouring heavily. My house-help, Meera, was worried and seemed preoccupied in her thoughts while trying to wrap up work for the day. My son who must be around eight or something at that time, stubbornly nagging me to get permission to go out to float his boats in the puddles. "When can I go outside mom?"

He was grumbling, "Mumma, it rains only for a few days in a year and I occasionally get the chance to float my boats. Sometimes I'm in school, and by the time school gets over, the rain stops. Sometimes, though it rains the whole night, it stops when I get up. It would have been so nice if there was only a monsoon season. Rains forever!! I could play in the rain whenever I wanted."

Hearkening to his wish, Meera started sobbing. "Beta, don't wish this." I gave her some tea and biscuits and when she became a little sober again, I asked her, "Why was she so upset?"

She shared her distress and worries with me. She had a family of eight and all adjusted in one room. Her in-laws, unmarried sister-in-law, and her family including their three kids.
"Didi, our room is not bigger than your kitchen. We sleep on the floor. Half of the family members sleep outside the room in the open area under the sky. Summers are fine but during winters and monsoon we have no other option but adjusting in that room only."

I asked her, "Where do you cook then?"

"During summers and winter, I cook outside the room but these days, I have to cook indoors only. First, I cook and once everyone eats, then we spread sheets on the floor and sleep. We are used to this Didi and I wouldn't have mentioned it, but yesterday it poured so heavily that water made way inside the room. I don't have dry clothes for the kids and no place and no grains to cook. Flour and rice also got soaked in the water. We can stay like this but I can't see my kids suffering." Meera again started weeping.

"The monsoon is a season of enjoyment for the affluent, but for poor people, it's a time of suffering Didi," she added. What she shared further, gave me goosebumps. Each time when her room is flooded, they prayed and waited till the rain stopped. The family used buckets to pump out the water.

I helped her by giving food for her family and some dry clothes. But a place to live? That was something I couldn't provide. My heart cried for her but was that sufficient? No.

There are many when it rains, they don't think about the weather, chai or music. They don't find it soothing. They run to save their belongings and find shelter for their children. They worry about their daily wages and whether they will get work that day or not. They worry about the next meal and God forbid if any of them fall sick.

While monsoon rains are essential for our crops, the poor drainage system in the cities of the plains and excessive interference with nature and spreading territories in the hills and jungles are costing us dearly. Many states reel under flood while there are places where farmers don't get enough rain for the crops.

While everyone looks forward to the monsoon in India, the season becomes an unmitigated disaster for many.

As a child, there is nothing more magical than the rains and as an adult, there is nothing more exciting than the reliving of memories of one's childhood. But what is magical for one, shouldn't be a nightmare for the other person.

Waiting to Fly

"You need not watch television whenever you are free. Why don't you try reading a newspaper? You are grown up enough to read a newspaper." I asserted to my daughter who was about to celebrate her ninth birthday next month.

She had been continuously switching between TV, tablet, and mobile for quite some time now. Being unable to go outdoors and meet friends had left the kids with limited options. Though she loves to read books, she isn't very interested in newspapers. I was trying to entice her into reading the newspaper.

For once, she agreed to read today on the condition that I would sit with her. Her dilemma was that she couldn't decide what to read or where to start.

I suggested she start with the sports page. She read a few paragraphs and wanted to go through other pages too. I was glad that she found it engaging.

After a few minutes, when I saw her reading the news, I stiffened in my seat. No, it wasn't due to what she was reading; she was trying to read political news and was asking too many questions, unable to comprehend most of it. I froze looking at the news in the next column, 'A Minor Girl Gang R***d'. What if she started reading it and asked me to explain it? What was I going to tell her? What impact was it going to have on her naive mind?

On the one hand, when we talk about educating young kids about 'Bad Touch' and 'Good Touch' and giving sex education, why was I worried?

Simply, I could not decide at that moment what would be more traumatic for a child. Telling her at this tender age that evil exists in our society or waiting for the day she would find out herself when she is probably a little more grown-up.

How much can you explain to a child who is just eight or nine years old? About sex? Especially non-consensual sex.

I'm just talking about the trauma when a child first learns and understands this heinous crime. The physical and mental trauma of a child who has actually endured it is beyond imagination.

How many of us change the channel when young children are around and such news is running on the television? I do. I have seen my husband feeling uncomfortable and changing the channel. We want to protect our daughter.

Why can't we feel safe watching the news or reading newspapers with our young children? That too in the safe confines of four walls of our own house.

Will there be a day when we can read, and watch, without fearing the deep impact it will have on young minds?

If so, that day would surely be safe enough for any girl to roam freely like a bird on the road, even in the dark of night, without fear of anyone.

I thought some of you would want to know what I did that day? Did she ask me anything? No, I didn't let her read any further. Cleverly, I diverted her attention to the next page and in that confusion, she lost interest in the newspaper. She was finished with the newspaper for the day.
I couldn't address the elephant in the room. I would not have been able to talk about the issue if she had asked about it. I didn't have the courage. Am I a weak mother?

Having said that I remember when I was young the same thing happened with me and my mother too. My mother was reading the news a bit loudly. She had this habit of loud reading. I wanted to read it too but she tugged the paper away saying this news isn't for you.

Like the entertainment industry, is there a need for censorship of the news too? With certain pages for the children and others restricted.

After decades, the dilemma still exists for parents.

CHAPTER SEVENTEEN

A Retail Therapy

We were on a short trip to Chandigarh for some work. We thought of utilizing this opportunity as a family outing amidst the COVID chaos. By this time, we were used to the pandemic, and people were trying to retain and incorporate this new normal in their 'normal' routine. To break the monotonous routine, we planned to do some sightseeing and shopping after our work was done.

"We are running short of time, there is no point in going sightseeing. Let's do some shopping for the kids." I suggested.

Kids were in dire need of some new cloths. I realized it only when I was packing for this trip. All their apparel was either worn out or appeared to have shrunken over time. The Kids have outgrown all their clothes in the last fifteen months and since they weren't going anywhere, shopping for new clothes hasn't been done at all. We had all been in our pajamas most of the time. At most in the Zoom Dress Code! Haven't heard of it? Oh! It's funny- a shirt with a tie and pajamas! Who was going to notice anyway?

Since H's birthday was approaching, he was on the

priority list. He reluctantly agreed to try one article, and as usual, the first article he tried was a perfect fit. No fuss about fitting, color, or design. When we suggested he should choose at least two t-shirts and one pair of trousers, he simply picked another color from the same lot. After much negotiation, he agreed to try a few more pieces, and finally, we were able to choose and buy something for him, though he didn't think it was necessary.

Throughout H's shopping time, princess A made it a point to remind us every half a minute that she was hungry, thirsty, or getting bored. My husband, as usual, was busy with his phone. Though, whenever he was asked for some suggestion, an enormous interest he exhibited. But at the mention of, "can you please take care of A?" He had a better suggestion, "Just ignore her." And all three of us tried our best to do exactly that.

Next on priority was shopping for my princess A, who always needs something. (female traits are visible right from birth) As we started moving towards the girl's section, we noticed a sudden spring in her walk. She led all of us, and by the time we reached the counter, few pieces were already chosen by her for the trial.

"Beta this is not looking good, just leave it," I suggested.

"Mumma you never know, it might look good. Let me try it."

How many articles did she try? I lost count after some time. We were surprised at her excitement. The hunger, thirst, and boredom were nowhere to be seen.

After finalizing four or five pieces, when we were waiting to make payments at the counter, she was ready with a fresh lot for another trial room visit. H was getting bored. I could sense it, but not once did he complain. Finally, we had to drag our princess forcefully out of the showroom. After some bribing and threatening, we were able to come out of that shop.

"So, we are done with shopping for the kids. Do you want to buy something for yourself?" I asked my husband. As usual, he had more than enough of everything and didn't need anything in the near future.

"If you want something for yourself, go ahead," he offered.

"No, it's ok. I already have a migraine, let's forget about more shopping," I blurted out. Immediately, I composed myself and rephrased when I saw this 'shop' I wished to check out. I popped an anti-migraine pill and continued on my shopping spree.

As I entered the shop, suddenly, princess A was again hungry, thirsty, and started getting bored. But this time, she had father's full attention. "You look around; I'll take her with me and buy something for her." When H also started to follow them, thinking he had no role in my shopping, It was beyond my threshold.

When I take so much interest in everyone's shopping, why do they try to escape when it's my turn? I will never understand.

Everyone got the hard glares, and H immediately withdrew and offered to stay back. My husband also apologized and showed me the brighter side. "She won't allow you to select peacefully. That's why I was taking her with me. I'll get a quick bite for her. You explore and choose and I shall join you back very soon."

Yes, he had a valid point.

I had shortlisted about ten to twelve sarees when he returned.

"I have shortlisted these; now you help me to zero in on one." He gauged the atmosphere as we tried to choose the best one and offered to let me choose two or three instead.

"Sure?" I asked.

"Never been surer," he replied.

I think choosing the one from the lot was more painful than paying for a few more. Then, there was a high chance I would regret not choosing the other one once we got home. So, we picked a few pieces (I don't want to disclose the number) and came out of the shop rather elated.

When H asked," how is your migraine mom?" I realized; I had forgotten about it. I had never felt fresher and more energized.

It's truly said, friends, never be in doubt, just shop till you drop. This is 'A Retail Therapy'. Who said that? I just experienced it!

CHAPTER EIGHTEEN

Dinner Table Chronicles

"Dinner is ready!" I called out from the kitchen.

"Give me five minutes, Mom. I'm just about to finish this topic. *Aap khana lagao,*" my elder shouted from his room.

I swear, I just saw him engrossed in his mobile a minute before when I crossed his room, and now, he wanted to finish the topic that should have been done over an hour ago.

"What's for dinner today?" asked my younger one, not moving an inch from her seat in front of the television.

As if the dinner menu would help her decide whether she was going to have her dinner or not.

I glance towards my husband, taking the clue he got up and retired to the restroom, stating, "Just coming in a minute, I need to freshen up first. *Khana lagao!*"

Within minutes the food was on the table.

On second call out, five minutes become two, younger one moves a little closer to the dining table, eyes still glued to the television screen and the man of the house was still in the bathroom, now on a call, probably from the hospital. He made sure the conversation was audible to me.

Clever man! Ensuring the alibi for his benefit.

"You know, I would have come earlier if it weren't for that urgent call," He grinned, a little sheepishly, though trying to gauge the atmosphere.

After two more calls and a warning, finally, all gathered at the dining table.

Our dining area is connected to the living room and television is visible from the dining table.

As we started eating, the animation channel changed to one of the prime news channels.

Courtesy of the man of the house.

Things were fine until *Her Majesty's* favorites animation was on. The moment it switched to the news, her verdict came, "Mumma says no TV while eating, *hai na, Mumma?*"

Now, the fate of TV depended on, whether I registered her plea or not, and 'whether I registered her plea,' depended on my husband's behavior over the last ten minutes.

The rest goes well. My family isn't picky about food except for few things, and I always made sure that if I cooked those few things an alternative was available.

After tolerating this for few days, there came a day when I cooked and left the kitchen, asserting, "When all of you gather and serve the food, just call me."

And that was my politest way of saying, "I'm fed up."

I switched on my show and waited for the, "*aa jao khana lag gaya.*"

Everyone behaved well that day and for the next mealtime.

Only to resume their NORMAL behavior soon after.

So, this is my crazy family, who eats together and stays together.

CHAPTER NINETEEN

Transformation to a New Life

Ever heard about Dragonfly?

In short-

Thick muddy bottom of the pond was inhabited by a community of water bug.

There, they scurried about unaware of the outside world and what it held. They were happy and contented.

Now and then, a water bug would cling to the stalk of a lily and laboriously work its way up and disappear from view for good.

All wanted to know, where they all go? So, after much discussion, one agreed to go up the stalk and return to tell where and why others went and what lies beyond their world?

Soon, on a warm spring day, the leader herself clung to the slippery stalk of a water lily. Slowly but steadily, she moved up, up and up. On reaching the surface, exhausted by her efforts, she dropped on a big round leaf.

After a long sleep, she realized that she felt different. She looked at herself, amazed at the transformation. She felt a great urge to fly, fluttered her wing nervously and rose high.

She, The Dragonfly, rejoiced in her newfound freedom, tried all kind of aerobatics and finally when landed on a lily leaf to rest, happened to look down at pond bed. Looking at the water bug community she remembered her promise and tried to dive. Alas! She was a dragonfly; she could no longer go to the pond bed.

We are just like them. We, babies, in the womb of our mother. I have just come out of my mother's womb. This is my story, but other babies wouldn't know, till they experience it themselves.

I was happy in my world when fate decided for me that I could explore further.

It was some time back when my heart had started beating and I had come to the life.

Ah! Life, it's a different and beautiful feeling but I was alone and couldn't see a thing; just felt it. It was dark everywhere but I could sense a reassuring warmth surrounding me and I was unafraid.

It felt like I dived in but couldn't swim, as I didn't have my fins, but I managed well and knew I'd eventually reach the shore.

Ah! I was tired, couldn't think for a while, and decided to sleep.

Yay! I had a nice sleep; seems some time had passed since then and now I was accustomed to my new surroundings but wait! My fins started growing or why was it looking like arms and legs to me?

Oh, God! Was I transforming into a mermaid? It was ok, but why, in this dark place seems like an oceanic to me? Let's see, I would love to explore it.

Time went on.

Whenever I flutter, I get a hearty meal. But at times some spicy things are thrown at me and I don't like them as they make me sick and I can't even get them out of my system.

Well, l can't see but someone talks and sings for me. It's pitch dark as the devil here. But that voice is so reassuring, and I feel loved!

I am getting bigger and bigger day by day and sometimes I feel suffocated but as I move, it feels better.

The speed by which I'm growing, I don't think this place is going to accommodate me for long.

I'm worried, is this end? Well, there is nothing I can do except to wait for the inevitable.

Today I'm feeling different, something is pushing me out of my home. I'm so accustomed to this place. Warm and reassured. I want to stay here, please don't push me.

I try to squeeze myself as small as possible. But someone is shouting, 'One More Push' again and again. An unknown force is adamant to through me out of my own home.

With a sudden gush, I come out of my world. It is so bright and radiant, maybe this is heaven!

Light is hurting my eyes, now I'm crying as I feel detached from my past world.

I'm being taken to someone they call 'Maa'... who is crying and laughing at the same time then I hear her. O God! Is this the same reassuring voice I heard in my previous life?

She holds and hides me affectionately in her bosom.

I'm surprised at my transformation as I breathe and inhale in her scent.

This is my second chance to live and I love it to the core and I would love to explore.

Though the umbilical cord is severed at the birth Emotional ties to remain forever. This is a bond that endures until the very last breath.

CHAPTER TWENTY

Gift of Equality and Respect

It was Sia's eighth birthday. Preparations were in full swing. She was very excited and so was her family.

Sia's last two birthdays could not have been celebrated amid lockdown restrictions. On her sixth birthday everyone did their best to cheer up her spirits with homemade cake and gifts bought, packed, and delivered online, yet it was nothing to match a celebration in the presence of one's friends. She so wanted to show off her long frilly gown and the new dollhouse. Anyway, it wasn't much fun playing with that dollhouse all alone.

Her parents promised her that her next birthday would be with friends, but when that could not happen, it left Sia even more heartbroken.

The only ray of hope during the lockdown was Bunty, the house-help Meena's son. He was so young at that time and family allowed her to bring him along when she joined them again after the first lockdown.

This year with dreaded hearts everyone just kept their fingers crossed. The day was near. The dress to be worn for the birthday, frozen theme cake and decoration, a gift from each family member, return gift for the friends, menu for the day, and also a magician for the magic show was booked for the day. An inflatable Mickey Mouse Bouncy Slider was placed outside in the lawn of the bungalow for the kid's entertainment, where the party was to be organized.

Meena was in much demand today. Everyone had something to instruct Meena.

Meena, have a look if the food is ready?

Meena, help with decoration.

Meena, stack return gifts on the table.

Meena, iron baby's dress.

So, on and on...

Meena too was very happy for Sia baby. How could she not be? She was such an angel. So kind and soft-hearted. She loved her son and she always let him play with her toys. But today Sia was too occupied to remember Bunty. All her school friends were about to come.

Meena was not herself. Her son, Bunty too wanted to attend Sia's birthday. But Meena was afraid he might create a scene in front of all the guests.

She knew she would get everything for him from the house. Her family too would get to have the feast. But at the end of the party, when she would finally leave after binding up everything. But four-year-old Bunty wanted to see all the celebrations. He hadn't seen such a decoration before. And the most fascinating was that mickey mouse bouncy slide.

Meena instructed him not to come out of the house till he is asked to.

Suddenly, she heard someone squeaking with happiness and she froze at her place. This was for sure Bunty. How did he slip out of the outhouse, where they lived. She had instructed her husband to keep him inside so he wouldn't come out of the house. She turned around to have a look and couldn't believe her eyes. There she saw Bunty, in new clothes, sliding on the mickey mouse. He was as much part of the party as other kids were. She lifted her eyes to look at her mistress, who smiled too. The gesture made Meena's heart swell with relief and joy.

Suddenly, her speed of working increased in a multitude of her joy. With springs in her feet, she could be seen serving and taking care of everyone.

It seems that Sia made it clear to everyone that Bunty was her friend and she wasn't going to celebrate her birthday if he wasn't invited. Everyone kept it a secret from Meena.

The gift Meena received today was priceless, a gift of equality and respect, embodying every child's right to honor and dignity, unclouded by the complexity of our society.

Meena was afraid that her son would be heartbroken but rather he was elated. She closed her eyes and prayed for the little angel Sia, "GOD, give her all the happiness that she can hold."

CHAPTER TWENTY-ONE

Choco Fudge Garden

My daughter was unhappy that day as her chocolates were out of stock. Her chocolate craving was increasing day by day. There wasn't a day when she wasn't binging on chocolates. So, I decided to not refill the stores. "She would throw tantrums, alright, I'll see," I thought.

She couldn't overcome the craving. "Mom, you could have ordered online," she fumed.

"Shona, you are eating too many chocolates these days. They are not good for your health and teeth," I advised.

"You knew I won't be able to sleep without having my chocolate dessert, mom," she complained.

"Okay, angel, come, and I'll tell you a story about the chocolate world. You would be able to sleep and you might have a chocolaty, sweet dream." I tried to cajole her.

This got her attention. And I narrated –

There was a boy named Raju and he was your age. He was very fond of chocolates. One day he found a beautiful stone and out of curiosity, he rubbed it.

You know what? A Genie appeared and asked, 'What do you want, sir?' Raju could not believe it.

He said, he always wished to visit the chocolate world. But he was not sure if it existed for real.

But his wish was granted.

"I can't believe it! I never knew about the chocolate world." Astonished Raju exclaimed as he reached chocolate world gliding on a cocoa tree sled.

He was looking at chocolate Mountains, Choco fudge garden, chocolate shake fountain, and Choco streams.

The Browne fairy introduced Raju to the inhabitants of this world.

They were all happy. All had brown chocolaty eyes which shone so bright.

Hazel, Beige, Auburn, and Umber all looked so cute. They all were on their weekly projects to show the visitors the chocolate world.

As it was Raju's first visit, they all took responsibility to show him around.

They first went on a trek to the mountain. They had to swim through a warm soothing choco-lava stream to reach the base of the mountain.

As they were climbing, they ate candies from the Choco Fir trees.

At the peak, they noticed a wandering cloud, and soon all were drenched in the milky Choco shower.

While they were coming down, they sipped Nutella drinks from the Choco fall.

They went to the Fudge Garden and ate cupcakes. In the center of the garden, a huge 'Death by Chocolate' was kept.

"It's all yours. You can have as much as you want," Hazel said to Raju.

Raju ate to his heart's content. Soon he was full and his tummy started aching. He wished to go back.

He was sent to the Choco tunnel station and as he entered it, he fell directly to his bed.

As he woke up, he was in his bed.

The whole day, he could taste chocolate in his drool.

My darling daughter slept after listening to the story. To her surprise, she was no longer craving chocolates.

She understood that too much of everything is bad. She promised to herself to eat them in moderation.

CHAPTER TWENTY-TWO

Nutsy and Munchy Getting Ready for Winters

"It's time to sleep, baby," I implored my daughter.

"Ok, Mumma, you too come and tell me a story, then." For a change, she quickly agreed.

"What do you want to listen to today? A fairy tale, a princess, or an animal's story? maybe squirrels, which we saw today at the park."

She squeaked like the one. "Do you know the story of a squirrel?"

"Yes! Mumma knows every story and about anybody." I spoke.

"Story of squirrel then." She snuggled into the crook of my elbow, tilting her head upward so she could watch my expression as I told her the story. I rested my head, slightly propped up on two pillows, as I started the story-

"There lived two baby squirrel friends in our nearby park on a tree in the extreme corner. Nutsy and Munchy. Both of them were neighbors and went to the same school."

"In the same bus?" my curious kiddo interrupted.

"No baby, they don't commute by bus. They hopped, ran and climbed from tree to tree, reaching their destination in no time. Their destination was a tree in the nearby park."

"They played together in the evening. It was so difficult for them to leave each other at night too.

"Like BFF?" she asked again.

"Yes. They always wanted to play and talk. Both of them had never-ending stocks of stuff to tell each other and ask the teacher.

This often interrupted the class and the teacher's flow of teaching. Their talkativeness was increasing day by day."

"Like me?" she asked with a naughty smile. The smile just reached the corner of her big brown eyes.

"Ummm... !! may be..." (she surprised me for having such insight and still adhering to the same behavior)

I continued, "Teacher had shared about this to parent squirrels and they tried to speak to them to improve their behavior but to no avail. No one was able to scold such young and cute little rodents. Moreover, whenever the teacher tried to be strict with them, Nutsy and Munchy squeaked, "please ma'am we won't talk next time" in such a manner, showing their cute beady eyes which would melt anybody's heart.

One day, they were being taught an important lesson in the class. How to find the way to the scattered hazelnuts through a maze and come back safely? They were also taught how to return to the source again in case they encounter a jackpot in the form of a heap of same which would last for the season?

The theory was taught in the class and later they were supposed to enter the maze and come out with hazelnuts safely and again to return to the spot quickly.

As usual, Nutsy and Munchy were busy in their chitchat and didn't listen to the lesson properly.

"Fir kya hua? Wo kho gaye?" (What happened? Did they get lost)

"Have patience baby!"

They went inside the maze confidently and searched the heap of hazelnuts. After all, they were bright little squirrels. They held one nut in their mouth and one each in their claws. Both of them wanted to be together and were constantly bumping into each other. They were also carrying more nuts than they could handle so they couldn't make it out in the given time. Also, as both of them were not focused while finding their way the first time, they couldn't make it at all on the second attempt.

That day they failed and were saddened. It was life's most important lesson which they failed. Without managing to find food efficiently they wouldn't be able to survive.

Nutsy and Munchy were miserable that day, not talking on the way back home and choosing not to play. The mother squirrels knew the reason as their teacher shared everything with them.

Their mothers hugged them and asked the reason. On getting some affection and sympathy they couldn't control their emotions and started crying.

Though they failed in the class lesson, they learned another important lesson about discipline and focus.

They got their lesson and promised to be a better student. Soon they learned all the tactics to search and hide their food.

"Why do they hide their food, Mumma?" I anticipated this from her.

They hide their food so other animals couldn't steal it. They pretend to dig and hide their nuts, but actually, they hid them elsewhere and would always remember where to find them later.

"They are smart!" She announced happily.

"Yes! Just like you." As I said this, she adjusted herself to a more comfortable position and was asleep in no time. A happy and content over her face.

CHAPTER TWENTY-THREE

A Dash of Red

A touch of kohl, a dash of red, and a small Bindi. This used to define my routine beauty care.

As eyes got hidden behind the thick glasses my shade of lipstick got brighter to compensate.

But who could think in their wildest dreams that someday, lips were going to be masked behind triple-layer and N95?

A mighty mask dared to change the definition of my beauty regime and tried to take away the secrets to my confidence. But I just could not let that happen and allow a tiny virus and a few layers of 4x4-inch cloth to succeed.".

After a dilemma of 'to wear it' or 'not to wear lipstick' beneath a mask, the former won.

So, when one day, I was getting ready to go to the hospital, my husband asked, "Why do you wear lipstick when you are going to wear a mask over it. It's not going to be shown to anyone?"

I fiercely replied, "Dear husband, please come out of your fallacies, who said that a woman wears lipstick to show it to somebody? I wear it to gratify myself. It gives me endurance and boosts my confidence. It's more important that I'm pleased with myself and I find and feel beautiful. Logon ka kya hai? Even if one says, 'You are looking awesome', I'm never sure, whether it's a true compliment.

Then, I wear it to please you as well. You see me. Right? I know you love me unconditionally, with or without a dash of rad, still when I get ready and see appreciation in your eyes, that look of yours linger with me the whole day.

No, no, no, don't stop me. I'm still not done.

It's also a secret beneath my mask which the other person doesn't know. It also gives a mysterious aura around me. look at me, I'm still a mystery you can't unfold."

My dear husband was tongue-tied. "I still don't know you enough darling, I think it will take more lifetimes to understand a woman," he replied.

I picked up my handbag and mask and left the house feeling confident and creating an esoteric aura around me.

CHAPTER TWENTY-FOUR

Borrowed Breath

To live, we need two square meals, eight to ten glasses of clean water but **twenty-one thousand times oxygen to breathe!**

The first two are voluntary actions. You make real efforts to eat and drink while breathing is an involuntary action done by your lungs and a few muscles. Day and night, whether awake or in your deepest slumber, you are sustained by oxygen, which, until recently, we thought came for free.

We have left no stone unturned in depleting that precious gift from the earth —'the air'—by attacking its lungs: the trees and forest. We still remember how nature took its vengeance by attacking our lungs with the tiniest and scariest living creature: the novel corona virus!

Battles are difficult when you can't see your opponents. Even you can't feel it. We only realized it once it had already established itself inside our bodies. By that time, we were stunned, and it was often too late to take effective action. While we were reeling in shock, it had already begun spreading through our communities, and we could not foresee who would be next?

Just as the Earth is warming day by day due to the rising carbon dioxide levels in the atmosphere, our own temperatures rose in response. It's a defense mechanism of our body. You couldn't even utilize the available atmospheric oxygen, gasping desperately for more.

That was when we borrowed some breath — udhar ki saansen, breaths we still need to pay back. That couldn't be managed at home. At times, we only needed high concentration-oxygen without machines, which could be managed at primary or secondary care centers. As soon as mechanical ventilation became necessary, intensive care units were needed.

It's not that India didn't have hospitals. It's like having enough food and groceries for your family for a month, but suddenly having to cater to a wedding party without knowing how many guests will arrive. And to make matters worse, every guest gathered at the dessert stall, fearing it would run out before their turn came.

Even if you managed to gather the groceries, did you have cooks to prepare the meals? Hospital beds are not just furniture, and medical expertise cannot be created overnight. It's a long struggle of at least ten years before you can make those beds effective.

We waited patiently to get through that phase, keeping our expectations low and saving our breaths. God forbid we should need to borrow breath and find there's none left.

In a world where breathable air has become a commodity to be purchased, and many struggle to afford it, Borrowed Breath is a story from COVID -19 era, when there weren't enough ventilators and when clean air had become a luxury.

CHAPTER TWENTY-FIVE

With the Blessings of a Cursed One

Wedding ceremonies and our honeymoon were over. We were about to get back to our workplaces, almost five hundred kilometers apart in two different cities. We, the newlywed amorous couple, still hadn't had enough of each other. I was miserable. There were still a few months before my husband could join me in my city after completing his tenure. Till then, we had no other option but to accept our fate and be a couple in a distant relationship.

Time flew, and soon we were reunited. Soon, my mother-in-law (MIL) joined us to help set up our household. After spending some time with us and setting up our household, my in-laws left, of course, after generously blessing us for our new life.

I conceived after a few months. When we broke the news of our pregnancy, they came to meet us. My MIL smiled rather triumphantly! Puzzled, I asked her the reason for her mysterious smile. After a few 'nothing, and kuch nahi hai,' she was unable to keep the secret-a secret that even I didn't know. She revealed the secret behind my pregnancy to me.

In North India, after the marriage of a son, they come in a group to bless the newly married couple. They sing, dance, and bless the couple for a happy and long married life. They also bless them to have offspring, especially sons. A few decades back, they used to come to bless the newborn male child but nowadays as people have just one or two kids, they have started to bless all the newborns irrespective of their gender.

After our wedding, when they visited my in-laws' place, we had already left for our workplaces. So, they couldn't bless us. My MIL was a little sad. So, they provided her with some 'blessed' rice grains and instructed her to sprinkle those grains in the corners of our bedroom and over our heads. "You will get good news within a year," they professed. My MIL did as suggested, but without our knowledge. To her surprise, we did give the 'good news' within one year of that.

"But mummy ji, I conceived because we planned," I tried to reason. "Their blessings made you think about planning your family," came her prompt reply. No one can contradict strong faith. With folded hands, I too accepted and felt gratitude for her faith.

Strangely, in many places in India, blessings from transgender individuals, who are forbidden to marry and bear children, are considered auspicious for starting married life and having children. A community that is not as blessed, we give them just a few gifts and some cash in return. But where are the dignity and respect they need?

They may not be as blessed, but have enough heart to bless everyone whose path crosses with theirs.

Such irony!

CHAPTER TWENTY-SIX

I'm a Little Teapot!

I was so hungry; I asked my house help to give me something to eat with my tea. I had come from my work and was exhausted and famished as I couldn't get time to eat anything throughout the day. Instantly, my daughter disappeared behind her toys specifically behind her kitchen set and reappeared with a tray with a cup and a plate. She stood in front of me while I lay down on the sofa, my eyes closed.

Sensing her near me, I opened my eyes to find her standing with a tray.

"What is it, Shona?"

"Mom, tea and sandwich for you. You said you were hungry."

I was too tired to play along so I proposed to her, "Shona, can we play later as I'm very tired and hungry right now?"

"I'm not asking you to play Mumma. Just have it because you are hungry, then take some rest. We can play later." I was touched by her gesture but still wasn't in the mood to be carried away by her proposal.

I asked her to keep the tray on the center table. While she was setting it down, the cup was knocked over.

"Oh! The tea has spilled." She exclaimed and ran to grab a duster to clean up the imaginary spilled tea!

As she cleaned, house help brought my tea and snacks, which I started munching on without realizing how much it would impact her.

She was so upset that I hadn't had the tea and snacks she made for me, even though they were imaginary.

I had noticed before that whenever kids play pretend, they truly live it. My son also played pretend games but not as seriously as my daughter did. At times, I worried. What if she lost distinction between reality and fantasy?

So, I researched and read about it and it turned out that pretend play is great for a child's overall development.

I had seen my daughter pretend to be characters from stories like Rapunzel, Cinderella, and Anna and Elsa. She recreated entire story or the episode of such a series with her friends. It keeps children engaged, increases vocabulary and social skills. This helps children appreciate relationships, understand characters' point of view, and comprehend behaviors, which is sometimes too complicated to grasp otherwise. This is important for a child's emotional competence and overall cognitive development.

Once I saw my daughter enacting Cinderella. I asked her if she knew what a stepmom meant? She said stepmom was simply a bad mom! I explained that 'stepmom' just means a mother who is not a biological, and being bad or mean has nothing to do with whether a mother is biological or not. A person's behavior depends on certain circumstances and how they perceive and react to them.

It's so rejuvenating to see them pretend play.

See Mumma, "I'm a bird and I'm flying!"

"Oh! I'm a tree and I'm rooted to my place!"

Sometimes she came to me pretending she was a cat and all I have to do was pat and stroke her.

And the most intriguing was when my son would say 'I'm a little teapot!' with one hand on his waist and the other crooked in the air like a spout.

Isn't it beautiful and simultaneously rewarding in so many ways?

I Wouldn't Touch It. Did I Mention Only in Your Presence?

My son was just a toddler at that time. We had joined a medical institute in Tirupati. My husband had already joined his department and I was planning to join after settling the things at home. We had shifted our base from North India and settling things was going to take some time.

We were provided with a semi-furnished residence on the campus. Of all the things there was a mini refrigerator that wasn't going to serve our purpose but I decided to use it for time being till mine got installed.

I placed my food processor on top of it so my son couldn't reach it.

The kitchen platform, which was the right place to keep the food processor, was well within my son's reach, and its knob fascinated him. He would play with it whenever he got the chance-off, on, off, on-turning it right, then left. I feared the knob would come off, so I placed it on top of the refrigerator where he couldn't reach.

Well, I was wrong. Who can stop a curious mind? He tried to reach it, adjusting his weight on his toes. Just a few centimeters more, he must have thought. I saw him doing it and tried to scare him. "Do not try to touch it. It might fall and you would get hurt." He nodded in understanding or I thought so!

A few days later, when I was busy with something, I heard a LOUD THUD! I hurried towards the sound. The food processor was lying on the floor, its parts scattered hither and thither. At that very moment, my little prince entered from the opposite direction, shouting "Kya Toota? Kya Toota?" (What has broken?)

I forgot the food processor and looked in his direction. My heart fluttered and then skipped a few beats altogether. It took only a few seconds for me to grasp the entire situation. But those few seconds were enough to give me a heart attack. (Only both of us were home).

Both of us looked at each other in utter scare. He poker-faced! At the untoward turn of the events, weighing what was going to happen next while simultaneously trying to comprehend my psychology!

And me? I was simply unable to decide whether to cry with joy at his cleverness or scold him for being such a spoilsport!

He was anxious but seemed fine otherwise. I asked him if he was hurt and that was the point, he must have seen some softness in my eyes. He started sobbing, pointing to multiple spots on his legs. Here, I'm hurt.

I examined him properly. He wasn't hurt. It was his tactic to avoid getting in to trouble. He was afraid to get scolded. Within a few minutes, he was examining the broken parts of the machinery.

It seemed he was playing with it standing on tiptoes. As soon as he realized that the processor had become unstable and was about to fall, he ran in the opposite direction to take entry again only after me.

Ishhh...So much from a two-and-a-half-year-old!

No matter how well we take care of our kids, there will always be times when they manage to steal that one moment which we might regret for the rest of our lives. If only we had done this. If only I hadn't left them alone for that one moment.

We are often too hard on ourselves. No one wants their kids to get hurt but they still manage to get hurt sometimes. And we are all judged for that one moment, especially mothers. I guess, we all learn from our mistakes and try to be more careful only to err at some other point.

But then if we were perfect, we wouldn't have been human! Right.

CHAPTER TWENTY-EIGHT

Essential Skill for Living

A few days back I was having backache. Though I had been experiencing it since morning, I still managed to do my routine chores, including fixing breakfast and lunch. But for dinner, my husband suggested to have some instant noodles, which he and my son could manage easily. That way I could continue with my rest.

When I didn't get up, even though it was past my usual cooking time. My daughter who was concerned for me till now looked a little worried. But her worry was for a different reason now.

Who would fix dinner?

A few times she came to me and asked how I was feeling? I told her the pain was the same as it had been in the afternoon. She looked a little disappointed.

Then she suggested to me, "Mom if taking rest is not helping, maybe doing some exercise would help to relieve your pain." I was touched by her concern.

I asked, what kind of exercise, did she think would help me to get my pain relieved?

"Maybe you could try cooking something for dinner. Cooking is also a form of exercise." She quipped with a matter of fact.

Though I was pleasantly surprised by her wit and the wisdom with which she expressed her worry, I would be lying if I said I wasn't hurt.

I have got a very caring family. There is nothing which I do out of compulsion. Our generation is fortunate enough to have multiple options when one doesn't feel like cooking or doing any house chores.

Suddenly, my thoughts drifted to my childhood. It wasn't like my mother didn't fall sick. But I don't remember a day when she was at home and didn't cook. Only on those unavoidable occasions when she wasn't at home, either my father managed, or we were left in someone's care, who would cook and take care of us.

There simply wasn't an option like fast food or instant meal, let alone the option of dining out.

When I look back, I can see and imagine, how difficult it would have been for my mother to manage home. With no house-help and no help from her husband and kids.

Their arrangement was as simple as 'I earn and you manage the house'.

In our family of six, I was the only female besides my mother. At that time when it was perfectly acceptable for males of the house not to help (no one expected them to) and since I was a bookworm and studious child, I was given liberty in the name of studies.

For my neighbors, I was that studious Sharmaji's daughter, every child hated for being compared with. At the same time, I was often given examples of other Sharma daughters who were perfect helping hands, ready to step into their mother's shoes, if the need arose. I always suspected that my mother had a green eye for those mothers. In our house, my mother was the only one who ended up taking on all the responsibility alone.

There were only two times I had to take responsibility for feeding the family: once, for a few days, when she had surgery for fibroid, and again, for a few months, when she fractured her wrist.

This second time was just before I left home to pursue higher studies. And the experience sure came in handy in some adverse circumstances, when the hostel mess got closed for a few days. That same experience helped me sail through my early married days.

When I got married my husband knew some basic cooking skills. Thanks to his time in the hostel. But slowly, it was me who made him dependent.

During the lockdown, everyone realized the importance of survival skills, and managing three square meals became the most essential one.

Coming back to that day, while my son and husband prepared instant food for dinner, I resolved to teach each of my family members the skill to survive the hunger game.

CHAPTER TWENTY-NINE

Happiness is Watching Innocence Blossom Around

A couple of years back, I attended my daughter's kindergarten sports day meet.

It was a sunny day in an otherwise chilly December. The tiny tots, all decked up in their thick track suits and warm inner layers, looked like the cutest little stuffed walking soft toys.

There were many events: lemon-in-spoon race, sack race, hurdle race, frog race to name a few.

My daughter was participating in an event where she had to carry a small bucket, fill it with sand from a tray at a defined spot along the way, and then run to the finish line. The total distance was no more than fifty meters, keeping in mind their short strides.

Participants were grouped in a set of ten. Soon, it was her group's turn and ten cuties stood at the start line with buckets in their hands. They were instructed to run at the sound of the whistle. As the whistle blew, a few children started running immediately while a few first ensured that their friends had started before they ran themselves.

My daughter, who started immediately as instructed, realized after taking a few strides that her friend had been left behind. She stopped, looked back, ran to her, held her hand, and then both of them ran together. On the way, they filled each other's buckets and finished last, holding hands and gleaming with pride, for not leaving each other behind.

Few other kids were doing the same.

Almost none of them wanted to win!

At least, not without sharing the experience with their friends!

Spectators, who had been cheering and clapping, now chuckled at their innocence, while mothers like me were getting emotional, filled with contentment at their kids' selfless love for their friend, a love that surpassed any competitiveness.

After the event, during the prize distribution ceremony, this beautiful virtue of children was given a special mention.

Some of those who received medals were too naive to focus on their victory, still looking for their friends or parents among the spectators.

One could see, that for them, being with friends was more meaningful than getting medals and accolades.

Such innocence and selfless love always fill your heart with happiness.

CHAPTER THIRTY

When is the Right Time to Decide, What I Want to Be?

We, adults, are so ludicrous at times.

A couple of years back my eight years old daughter was doing her homework. She was required to write an answer for *"what she wanted to be when she grew up?"*

She was a little puzzled and didn't want to answer this question.

"What is the problem beta?" I inquired, not understanding her confusion.

"Mumma, I'm not sure what I want to be yet? I haven't decided yet." She revealed her dilemma.

"It doesn't matter. You can write anything, like doctor or engineer, for now. You can decide later when you grow up." I tried to reason out as a matter of fact.

Her reply left me perplexed. "No Mumma, then this answer will be wrong. So, I don't want to attempt this

question as of now." She said firmly.
I was speechless for a few moments.

On one hand, I couldn't stop admiring my kiddo for having such a clear outlook on such a complex topic; on the other hand, it left me pondering two things; one, the question itself, and the second, the elusive answer I provided.
When we don't consider them competent enough to take the smallest decision for themselves at this tender age, we want them to decide what they want to become even before they complete their first decade of existing on this earth.

Wonder why do most middle-class parents want their children to study medicine or engineering? Unknowingly, we impose our dreams on them and when we keep saying the same thing since their childhood, they start considering it their dream. Shouldn't we allow them to explore the world first so they can decide, unbiased, what they want to be?

Often kids are influenced by their teacher and they want to become a teacher in their initial school years. My kiddo is so influenced by her mom that she is sure about one thing that she wants to be a mom. Sure baby!

She is already doing her homework for that. She wants to learn cooking, so her kids are well-fed. She does not believe in outsourcing parenting and whenever she is a little impressed about my way of parenting, invariably asks for details and seems to take notes. I wonder!

I don't know what the future has in store for her. Right now, she should enjoy today and explore without worrying about tomorrow. I'm sure, she will grow up to be a kind person and choose the profession she would love.

CHAPTER THIRTY-ONE

Danger Might Not Look Dangerous

They advised me not to go out in the dark. They also warned against being in deserted places. The reasoning was simple: it's dangerous to be alone. More so if it's dark. Both situations, they said, would make me vulnerable- to being robbed of not just my belongings but also my sense of safety, my self-esteem, and my dignity.

But it wasn't either when someone groped me at the railway station. It was the middle of the day and the platform was huddled with passengers departing for and arriving at their destinations. Quite a few of them had also come to say goodbye or receive someone. There was a comforting normalcy in the chaotic movement of people, bags, and trains. In that moment, I was supposed to be safe. But safety is an illusion, and it shattered in an instant.

I don't know which category HE fell into- the man who groped me.

They also proclaimed a certain kind of people to be dangerous, depending on their outer appearances. They had to be well-built or in disguise. A way distinct to be called NORMAL. Just look at them and you will sense danger!

Really?

HE was none. An old eightyish male with a spine not so straight. He had the audacity to meet my eyes after committing the disgusting act-his own eyes were unflinching, unashamed.

I was too shocked to react. Perhaps I didn't even know how to react or what to say?

Who would believe me? I questioned myself. I knew the world would doubt me back. He can't even walk straight. How could you accuse such an old man? Probably you imagined it or maybe it was by mistake. Look, it's so crowded. However, one tries, cannot pass through without getting touched and without brushing the others.

Anyway, in a fleeting second, while these thoughts crossed my mind he disappeared into the crowd. But not before giving me a second glance, winking, with a triumphant smile on his face!

I was in utter shock, trying to process and digest the incident. All those warnings about danger in the dark or in deserted places suddenly felt irrelevant.

I had to rethink. Where was I truly in danger? When I was alone or in the crowd, in the dark or broad daylight?

Somewhere in our life, most of us must have faced this. Many of us have suffered silently and if at all some could muster the courage to share with parents or someone dependable, didn't get the support or advice. While raising awareness and educating your child is essential, it is equally important to watch for signs of discomfort, especially if they are too scared to share their thoughts. When they finally find the courage to open up, trust and support them.

CHAPTER THIRTY-TWO

Stop and Smell the Roses

How I wish I had a pause button; I would press it and appreciate the life in front of me.

"Really! 'Stop and smell the roses' is just a cliché." My inner voice mocked me.

"As if you know?" I shot back.

"You can slow down if you want to. The pause button is right in front of you. Try looking past your ambitions. Can you do that?" my inner voice retorted.

For once, I was astounded. I knew it was the truth. When do we get the time to pursue what makes us happy and appreciate what we have? When we were young, our parents constantly reminded us to focus on our studies saying, "Once your life is set, you will have enough time to do what you like."

I have been saying the same to my children as well.

Life is measured through the merits and ranks. We forget to pause and smell the roses in between. We are valued in society for our higher ranks. Yes! We do get recognized for our good deeds and virtues but usually, that is short-lived.

I'm done with my education; my career and family life are on the track. I'm on the latter half of my life. Had I got time to pursue my hobbies till now? A big no. How are my kids going to find the time for that when I'm still waiting for the *right time* to smell the roses? These days, we pursue our hobbies as if they are a contest. To get the certification, to get the medals and accolades. When was the last time I did something just to please myself? I don't even remember.

I wanted to learn to drive. I learned it when I was required to drive to complete my daily errands, not for my pleasure. I hadn't had enough time to learn driving, till I needed it.

Even exotic vacations are decided to boost our egos rather than alleviate our hunger to know the world better or simply to be close to nature and feel it.

Now when I'm on the other half's side of my life. I just took a moment to think about what pleases me.

1. I always wanted to learn to play a musical instrument. I just enrolled myself in the lessons.

So what if I don't understand the music? That won't deter me from trying to learn or understand it.

I remind myself often that I'm doing it for myself, not for certification. It doesn't matter if my notes aren't perfect; it's fine as long as I enjoy them.

2. I love to sing. I don't even remember the last time I sang like no one was listening. I'm trying to recapture those moments and live them in the present.

3. I try to focus on the positive things.

4. I make it a point to enjoy my morning tea and have it before it gets cold.

5. Other things can wait, but I do like to literally stop and smell my roses. In the morning, I go to my small garden and talk to my green friends, and take a moment to admire their beauty.

Gratitude and satisfaction are the keys. Count an event, a behavior, or an object and find a positive connection to it. Connect to nature, connect to yourself, connect to the present, appreciate and count your blessings.

You will feel the fragrance all around you.

CHAPTER THIRTY-THREE

Freedom from Self-expectation

This happened a decade ago. It was my birthday. It was a mid-week day and one of the busiest days for both my husband and me. I came back home from my work while my husband promised me to come back soon. But he couldn't keep his promise. We hadn't planned any extravagant party; just a simple dinner with our immediate family. But due to his busy schedule, it didn't happen. As I was also a little tired, I fixed a simple dinner and was about to retire for bed when he returned from his work.

For me, the day had started in a delightful mood but ended on a furious note. His behavior, as though nothing had happened, added fuel to the fire, and I ended up ruining both my and his evening.

I took this extremely personally and turned cold towards him. How dare he ruin my perfect birthday evening?

After some reflection, I had a huge epiphany: he hadn't ruined my evening. It was my own negative thoughts, entirely created by my expectation of how he should have behaved.

I had anticipated that he would take time off from work, but he couldn't. He had apologized when he called, but I expected more. After all, it was a big day for me, and he couldn't meet the standards I had set.

In reality, I was the one responsible for ruining my mood.

The next day, he made up for the previous day and I had a nice time. Only if I had fewer expectations and had some patience, my birthday evening would have been much better.

This is just one example of how expectations from other people can cause pain and suffering. There are many examples in our lives and some are so common.

Expectations from our elders, our in-laws, and from our kids for that matter.

The first thing we do in any relationship is setting up expectations. Isn't it?

So, this was the story of expectation from 'others' in a relationship and I understood and addressed it to an extent.

In the coming years, I was about to experience the worst.

The expectation from oneself!

Believe me, however, we may not want to say it aloud, but the expectation from self is hardest, just like motherhood and when both come at the same time, no one can help.

This is the most devastating BUT the most common combination.

When I had my first child, I wanted to be the 'perfect mom'. I sat standards for everything.

Yes! I was a 'doctor mom' and no one knew better than me.

My child would not get bottle-feed. Period.

My child will have 'n' number of feeds. Period.

His sleeping time, his waking up time, I wanted to control everything.

Result?

He was hungry most of the time.

Soon I needed to return to work. So, I was training to feed him with the help of a spoon rather than a feeder.

Most of the time feed was getting spilled rather than satiating him. A vicious cycle formed: a hungry child, feeding attempts, spilled feed, more crying, and both of us having disturbed sleep. And repeat.

The harder I tried the worse it got.

Then, my gynecologist intervened. She said, **"Motherhood is forever. Take it slow as it is a marathon, not a sprint. Don't set ideal situations. It's a hard job, and the rewards come in the moments. Stay sane enough to enjoy those moments. If your ideal situation isn't working, try for a less perfect one."**

I started my son on the feeder. Within a week his schedule was set. He was no more a hungry and cry baby. He was sleeping peacefully, so was I.

Yes, I had to take care of his feeder's sterility, that was worth it and way better for both of us.

For my second baby, I was less fussy in setting rules for her and I went easier on expectations from myself, and believe me she was proportionately a lesser fussy child.

Motherhood isn't a competition. Step out of the race to be the best mother- your child loves you for who you are. Don't try to change your identity in the zest of being the best. They don't want the best mom-they want a happy mom.

Then, I don't want to suggest that you lower your expectations. You hope for the best outcome but don't get carried away with negative thoughts when it doesn't work out your way. Do not try to control the way people think, react, or feel.

Don't set unrealistic standards for yourself. Remember, there are many ways to get things done-if one method doesn't work, try another.

Your feeling of happiness should not depend on the actions and reactions of other people. The world owes you nothing.

Get freedom from expectations to avoid misery, which is entirely avoidable, and in your hands.

Live in the moment, try to be open to any reaction from others, and your happiness should depend on your thoughts and beliefs.

Don't be harsh on yourself.

I manage my expectation of others and myself before they manage my life. I feel liberated.

And you?

CHAPTER THIRTY-FOUR

The Egg-cidental Confession

I belong to a typical vegetarian family where even the use of onion-garlic was forbidden during my grandmother's reign. As my father moved out for studies, he started having onion and garlic. It's not that he wanted to, but it was to adapt to the limited availability of cooked food. Later he settled there only as he took a job in the city. My mother too was from the same *satvik* background, and she had learned to use onion and garlic after marrying my father.

Subsequently, we were also made to eat eggs for their nutritional value, though we never had non-vegetarian food.

I still remember that during my childhood, we would hide or throw away every forbidden thing whenever my grandparents visited us.

When I got married, the scenario was almost the same for my mother-in-law. Onion was not forbidden but rarely used. Garlic was strict no and eggs and nonveg food?

Even if you talk about it and my mother-in-law would run to take a shower again.

It's not like that I loved eggs but for the nutritional value and ease of cooking it, I preferred to have eggs.

So, we followed the same protocol: have it when you're alone and finish it off or throw it away before the in-law come to stay with you.

There were occasions when they suddenly planned to visit us, and as a rule, we always got rid of the remaining eggs first to prepare the house for their stay.

And we never got caught till that day...

My son was at that age when kids love to share everything and every minute details that had happened with them recently. So, this time other than hiding or finishing off eggs, we also had to prepare our son so he wouldn't share the details accidentally.

"Beta, when dada-dadi visit us, we won't eat eggs. So, remember two things: first, don't ask for eggs while they are staying with us, and second, don't tell them that we eat eggs." I tried to make him understand. He nodded his head that he got the point and agreed to not share with them.

I remembered to remind him just before they arrived and I think I underestimated him.

The moment my mother-in-law entered the house he spoke up everything right in front of us. I froze at my place.

She didn't believe him at first, so she cross-questioned him. "How do you take it?"

He was quick to reply, "Boiled or omelet."

She again didn't believe and asked, "who makes it?"

"Mumma" came the reply.

Then, came the next volley, "who else eat it?"

"Everyone."

"Your Mumma too."

"Yes."

That was it. She didn't say anything, but I ran around like a headless chicken, being extra sweet, trying to compensate for the damage already done.

My MIL just asked, "I hope you have a separate set of utensils for that purpose."

That I had because I knew she wouldn't like to use those utensils for herself. So, irrespective of whether she knew or not, I respected her beliefs.

This was just one of the many occasions when my son put me in an embarrassing situation.

Only one thing that lessened my guilt a little was that my MIL didn't mind much if her son and grandson ate what was forbidden for the lady of the house.

So, I told myself to just chill! Now I didn't need to worry about getting caught.

Have you ever been in such situations?

CHAPTER THIRTY-FIVE

Hearts and Veins Entwined

We were just a few days into our nuptials. Henna on my hands was still in its brilliant hues. I remember that evening as vividly as if it were yesterday.

He caressed the back of my left hand with his right. His feather-light touch traced from my crimson-painted ring fingernail to the ring we exchanged.

His eyes sparkled brighter than the diamond on my finger, as his fingers traced each knuckle. He held my hand gently, caressing it with the soft cushion of his thumb. My eyelids grew heavy, a quite sigh slipping from my lips. My body still unaccustomed to his touch, responded too soon.

His lips parted a little. Maybe he was about to confess his love once more. "Such a nice vein. Just perfect for cannulation." He blurted out absent-mindedly, looking at one thin but prominent vein in my hand.

I got the shock of my lifetime!!

"What are you talking about? Of all things, you're thinking about piercing my vein?"

"Hey, isn't that what I'm doing? Day in and day out." He tried to justify himself.

Needless to say, he was about to enter his MD final exams. The final year of residency. In his branch of medicine, of all the worries, the foremost was to maintain a patent venous line to administer all the medication and fluids to the patient. So, they always have a good eye for a prominent vein for the cannulation.

Though I felt a little weird at that time I was proud as I got to know him better with time. How dedicated he is to his profession and how kind-hearted he is towards humanity!

Now, after more than two decades together and weathering many challenges, my admiration and respect for him have only grown.

He is my favorite doc and my better half. Thank you for being the best part of my life- my everything!

CHAPTER THIRTY-SIX

Who is 'The Genius'?

The urge for extracurricular activities like craft and art reaches its peak when kids have an exam the next day. All ideas that remain dormant for the rest of the year suddenly start popping up. And they need to address them immediately, otherwise, you know, the sky may fall down.

About exams? Anyways exams come and go four times a year, so should not be taken too seriously you know! Even if one scores a hundred percent, the first position cannot be guaranteed. Almost a dozen kids in each section are going to score the same marks. Schools no longer believe in the ranking system. They provide grades. And so many kids are in the same category. So, it doesn't matter much.

No, my darling daughter didn't say all this. She just said, "I'll do it, Mom. You worry too much."

But I still read between the lines.

Genius!! Yes, that's me.

The fashion design bug had been wriggling under her skin since morning. She wanted to make dresses out of balloons for her dolls.

"You can do whatever you want once your exams are over." I tried to negotiate with her.

"But you always say this. You never let me do what I want. Moreover, I will forget the designs by then." She threw tempers.

Half the day passed, and she didn't study anything effectively. She was still trying to coax me to get her way.

I evaluated the situation and permitted her for half an hour. No doubt the outcome was good. But still, it was her social science exam the next day, not fashion design.

Finally, satisfied after designing the clothes out of balloons for her doll, she came to show me the results.

She wasted another quarter of an hour more asking for compliments and appreciating her work herself. Then came the triggering question, "When can I do it again?"

My patience flew out of the window by then.

I reprimanded her. Slightly intimidated, she attended to her abandoned books and notes.

Only to get hungry after a while. Then started the vicious cycle of going to the loo, having water, staring in blank space!

Soon the evening approached. Man of the house was back from his work. She was yet to start her revisions.

Look at her! She hasn't done anything today. Look at her, what was she doing the whole day? I showed him and he threw appreciating glances towards me.

"You're a genius. I know you have a plan B in place." fast came the reply.

The next two hours passed, sitting with her spoon-feeding the chapters she was weak.

She slept satisfied and prepared for her exam.

While retiring to bed, I was thinking, who is the genius. Me, or the one who got her way, or the one who played along and made use of it by lauding me for having a plan B?

CHAPTER THIRTY-SEVEN

Friendship Beyond Words

Happy birthday to you
Happy birthday to you
Happy birthday Dear Aadi
Happy birthday to you...

It was my son's third birthday. We were on the way to the venue where we had organized for his birthday bash. And this was what he sang rather shouted on the top of his voice. Throughout the twenty-minute drive to the venue.

No, his name isn't Aadi.

Confused?

Aadi was his best friend.

As we were at that place for a short period only. And they haven't met since we moved from that place, leaving behind their friendship and other fond memories. It has been fifteen years. But it still brings a smile to our faces. I realized the depth of their bond that day when, instead of celebrating his own birthday, he kept wishing Aadi.

Aadi, short for Aditya, was a Malayali boy who spoke only Malayalam.

Hailing from Uttar Pradesh our mother tongue is Hindi. At the age of two and a half years, my son joined a kindergarten. He spoke and understood only Hindi with limited English vocabulary.

We had joined a medical college at Tirupati. A Telugu-speaking state. Where two toddlers met. One spoke Hindi, the other Malayalam.

"Do they talk? How do they converse?" I often asked the teacher.

"They speak their languages, but they understand each other perfectly," the teacher said with a smile. "Friendship doesn't need a language. Just like love, it can be felt even without speaking." She added further.

I occasionally ask my son now, if he remembers him? He did initially. He missed him immensely, but memories eventually fade. To the extent that he doesn't even remember his countenance. Just a vague familiarity with the name 'Aadi' persists, something etched in his heart forever. And that will remain with him for the rest of his life. After all, he was his first friend.

This is for you, my Sonny boy. The world is small. I'm sure as you explore the world and happen to come across a Malayali guy called Aditya, you are surely going to ask, "By any chance were you at Tirupati at some point in your life?"

Emotions transcend languages and boundaries. Just as love finds hearts across nations, so does hatred. No matter what we speak or write, may the language of love prevail and grow in each heart.

CHAPTER THIRTY-EIGHT

Sleeping is a Waste of Time: Naptime Negotiations

It was a Sunday. I was tired of wrapping up the pending work of the week simultaneously fulfilling the demands for something special, as it was a Sunday. You know it's the basic right of the family to have something special on Sundays. I too don't mind but you know a few times things just get unmanageable.

A demanding youngster and an even more demanding grownup (read husband) are quite enough to add to the already mismanaged weekend.

"Mom, please come and play with me."

"Mom, please can we go to have an ice cream."

It wasn't his fault that he wanted my attention. Sundays were the only days when I was at home for the whole day. So, when he asked me to sit with him, I suggested why don't we take a nap together.

"No, I don't want to sleep. I want to have fun. Sleeping is waste of time and who likes to waste time on Sundays?" he stated as a matter of fact.

Really? I didn't know sleeping was a waste of time.

So, I rephrased myself, "I'm a little tired, beta. I want to lie down for some time. You can just sit by my side and we can talk. What do you say?"

He agreed with a rider that he will only sit and I would not try to coax him into sleeping.

Though I agreed, this was exactly what I had in my mind.

Even one uninterrupted hour was enough for me to wrap up a few things that I wanted to get ready for the coming week. Chopping a few vegetables, ironing some dresses for the coming hectic mornings to name a few.

I patted my back for my intelligence. But I forgot he was my child and has inherited some of my traits.

With great cajoling, he agreed to lie down with me. I offered my crook of the elbow for a pillow to him. He accepted but kept on talking gibberish.

I bribed him to let me take a nap for five minutes in exchange for an ice cream treat in the evening.

He granted my wish. But he kept on looking at the wall clock.

"Mom five minutes are over. now get up," He declared after a minute as he didn't know to read the time.

"But I wasn't even asleep yet, I was still trying to sleep."

"OK... then you let me know when you fall asleep. I will wake you up five minutes later."

"Hey Bhagwan Ji, bacha lo mujhe!" I cried.

"Why don't you close your eyes?" I demanded.

"No, I would not. You want to make me sleep."

"Just close your eyes, this time I instructed him a little sternly. I can feel you gazing at me. I'm not able to sleep."

He closed his eyes to squint every few seconds to check on me.

This was the last thing I remembered before dozing off.

My husband told me later that he came out with a triumphant smile and declared, *Mumma mujhe sulana chahti thi, maine unhe sula diya.* (Mom wanted to make me sleep but I made her instead).

A couple of years back, when he used to fall asleep while studying, my younger one would come running. "Mumma, Bhai is sleeping, not studying." I shushed her, I knew he wasn't wasting time, he was recuperating to give his best shot.

Poles Apart, Yet Same

People say that two kids are poles apart. But I didn't believe them till I saw it for myself.

My older one never wanted to slip into new clothes. Even for parties, he preferred his pajamas over formal clothes. After a lot of coaxing and cajoling, he would have some mercy and oblige us by agreeing to wear a relatively new pair. Usually, that moment would only arrive after a lot of tantrums, drama, and meltdowns.

Whereas other kids would arrive at the party dressed up, he would show up in his usual attire. Still, we were grateful and thank him and our stars for not making an appearance in his second skin. He had one particular "night suit" that was very dear to him. He would sit in front of the washing machine so he could take out that night suit to wear again. We called that piece his "second skin." An hour before any party, that was what we dreaded most.

Shopping for new clothes for him was equally terrifying. Just imagine shopping for a cherubic, innocent-looking tot who wouldn't fit into the clothes for his age. By height, he needed one size smaller and by girth, two sizes bigger. It was pointless to buy any clothes for him without first trying them on to calculate options for folds and alterations.

And he would not agree to a fitting!

I'm not ashamed to admit that a lot of drama would follow on his end and a lot of coaxing followed by intimidation on ours.

This continues to this day, with varying levels of severity and different handling methods from both sides. Do I need to mention that he is a grown man now?

Years later, when we were blessed with our daughter, my first thought was, "I can shop for her to my heart's content." I was hoping she would be poles apart from her brother. That means no drama or tantrums while shopping or before a party. She would be happy to wear new clothes and even happier to try more.

Yes, she was, but drama was inevitable!

I vividly remember the first time we went shopping with her. We wanted to buy shoes for our son. She was still a toddler. We were choosing shoes for him when she disappeared for a while. When I searched for her, I found her at the next counter, proudly holding one shoe in each hand. Almost twice her size and from two different pairs. She wanted them for herself and was quite upset that no one was paying attention to her.

She was perfectly fine with having two mismatched shoes and insisted that the size was just right. When we finally left the shop, we noticed a dozen eyes full of sympathy and lips curved in a smile following us to the exit. Our son carried his shopping bag, my husband carried our toddler with flailing arms and legs, and I carried her old shoes in my hands.

This is just one of the many such instances. At times we won, and at others she did, when we had to buy certain things amidst much drama, which she later used just to play with.

Many times, we just took her measurements and avoided taking her with us to buy her dresses. The same with toys. Whenever she accompanied us, she seemed to memorize the locations of many toys, later demanding them on different occasions. She would tell us some weird descriptions of some location in the shop. Just imagine those times when the shopkeeper rearranged his items, and we were trying to locate a specific toy from a particular shelf!

So much for being poles apart yet the same in our experiences. Full-on tantrums and drama!

One is east, the other is west. My world revolves around them. My rising sun and shining moon!

"He is a grownup lad. He will look after his sister; you need not worry." People predicted when we decided to walk again on parenting journey almost after a decade. There were moments when he didn't approve and questioned our parenting methods. He was only ten and we had to remind him that we only have reared you.

They have the same sibling rivalry as siblings who are almost the same age. However, the moment you confront one, the other will step in to support.

Please, Get Married Once Again

"Mumma, where did I come from?" Every parent faces this question in their early days of parenting. The wording might vary, but all kids are inquisitive and the first thing they want to know is. 'Where did they come from?'

A tremendous task for any parent is to convince them successfully.

Now, we parents have a few options

'You came from mummy's tummy,' is usually the first choice.

'We brought you from the hospital,' comes next.

Some mischievous parents might say, "We BOUGHT you from the mall," and a quite costly affair you were.

If they are satisfied with that answer, consider yourself lucky. But in most cases, be ready for the next volley, that too at the most embarrassing and unexpected situation.

Embarrassing their parents is, after all, their birthright.

But what if your child has already assumed the answer or this never even had the question in the first place.

That's where my daughter comes in!

One day, she came to me with both her hands on her hips and confidently instructed, "Mumma, you get married again." She caught me completely off guard. Suddenly, she had my full attention.

"What has he done now to make his little princess think about abandoning him at this age?"

I cursed my husband in my mind before asking her the reason, "I'm happy in my marriage. Are you angry with Papa?"

"No, Mumma, you and Papa should get married once again," she insisted.

Oh! I sighed in relief. "We would think about it on our silver anniversary." I said, assuming she'd seen someone redoing the vows.

But she wasn't done. "That would be too late. I want the baby now!!" She dropped the bombshell.

Completely taken aback, I asked her "What does that even mean?"

"You got married once and had Bhai. Then you got married again to get me. Please, pretty please, get married once again." she pleaded with folded hands.

"One doesn't have to get married to have kids... No... I mean to say... Umm... I floundered to come up with the right words. One doesn't have to get married each time to have a child." I completed my sentence with quite a difficulty.

I regretted my words the moment they left my mouth.

I wasn't ready but as expected the question was immediately barbed at me, "Then how are babies made? I thought babies were born when you get married."

I was speechless! How did she even come to that conclusion?

In our country, children are almost always born within wedlock. This simplifies many of the complications that may arise in an otherwise situation.

What we see regularly, they consider normal. That's how little kids perceive the world. They observe their surroundings and overhear the conversations. They don't need any special explanation. However, we try to be careful and secretive.

But in the coming time, relationships are becoming a little complicated. Live-in relationships and a single parent with a surrogate child are being common day by day. The trend is likely to increase in the future.

While these arrangements offer a lot of freedom to the parent/ parents, we still need to consider how they will impact a child's mental and psychological development.

CHAPTER FORTY-ONE

A Tale of Two Albums: His and Hers

'There is so much in the window but nothing in the room'

I read this phrase quite some time ago when technology was on its way to making humans its slave. I might not have comprehended the depth then but today it holds so true.

When my son was born, we made it a point to take his photographs often, aiming to complete a roll every month.

Then the excitement of getting those pictures printed and watching them again and again, each time reliving those moments. Those were mostly candid pictures because, with limited photographs per roll, we couldn't afford many attempts to get that perfect shot.

This ritual went on for the first year. One album for each month! Later as he grew up, he was always on the run. The frequency of chances to get him clicked became rare. Only on occasions when he was clinging to one of us or was sleeping. A few times we even bribed him to get that one click.

He was camera-shy, much to our disappointment. As new parents, we always wanted to capture a photo of him...

A few years later, we bought our first digital camera. We were so happy as we could capture as many pictures as we wanted to get that one perfect shot.

Although we intended to get the best pictures printed, somehow that moment never quite arrived. No one seemed to care for one.

Until...

During Covid, when I was on sabbatical, I had plenty of time to spend as I pleased. My daughter and I were going through the old albums. She was extremely disappointed going through those albums. She had quite a few complaints and issues.

1. None of the pictures were of her:

2. Her brother, when young was cuter than she imagined. (She thought all the cute baby pictures were hers).

3. Lastly, there were many pictures of three of us, where she couldn't find herself. My darling daughter often forgets that for a full decade before she decided to arrive and upheave him of his rights, her brother had a monopoly at our home.

Looking at one such photograph, she cried, "I wish to tear this picture apart. It makes me so sad. I never thought you could be so happy before I was born. Sob...

Sob... Dumbfounded, I didn't know what to say?

I tried to reason out with her, "you have so many pictures. Alone as well as with us. Most of the time your brother had clicked them. There isn't any reason to be envious."

"But all of them are either on the phone or computer, I don't have a single printed album that belongs solely to me." *'But all are in the windows and nothing in the room'.* She reminded me of the phrase that I read years back.

So true!

She is just the opposite of her brother. A camera-friendly, ready to pose even in her sleep. While we have countless folders of her photographs, we didn't have a single printed album.

I promised her a beautiful album of her own very soon. On her next birthday, the album was one of her gifts.

CHAPTER FORTY-TWO

The Night He Met With an Accident and Fled From the Scene

There was a thunderstorm outside. That night the sky was roaring like anything. Other than the thunder, you couldn't hear anything. But I heard it. A mongrel was growling nearby. There must be a stranger.

A stranger!! The mere thought made my blood run cold.

Suddenly the whirring sound of my AC and TV came out to a halt. There was pitch dark everywhere. I struggled to find the switchboard to put the lights on. By chance, the light that was switched on wasn't supported by the inverter. I cursed myself for choosing to go into a power-saver mode on that particular day. I don't know what difference it would have made to my electricity bill or global warming. But the moment definitely scared the hell out of me.

I know, I could use my phone light. But it too wasn't in my hand at that time. Tracing my steps to the switchboard was easier than finding the phone.

Power cuts during thunderstorms are normal. But that day I couldn't take it as normal.

I was waiting for my husband who went to attend to an emergency call at the hospital. Then only my phone rang. He had called to inform me that he was on his way back home. I wanted him to wait till the weather was a little better. But that day he didn't give a buzz.

"I am too tired and sleepy to wait any more and need a good sleep. I can reach home in ten minutes and sleep peacefully in 'my' bed," he said.

Who wouldn't? It was almost midnight. He must have been exhausted, and hungry. I didn't have the heart to importune so let him proceed. Though it wasn't safe to go outside that night, he sounded desperate. The hospital wasn't much far from our residence. And I thought he was right. One can take a nap in a doctor's room but that cannot match the comfort and peace of your own bed.

I also wanted to sleep snuggling beside him. I felt guilty about being in the comfort of my home. Warm and sated. "Please go ahead with your dinner, do not wait for me. I might not come back till early in the morning," he had instructed before leaving.

I knew as he was coming back so would eat at home only. Fixing his dinner quickly, I waited for him.

It had happened so many times in the past but today it was different. I was worried for some unknown reason. I just wanted him back. Safe.

I was pacing and peeped through my window several times before I noticed his car entering the porch. I saw him opening the main gate and getting back in the car. I ran outside to get the shock of my life. His windscreen was shattered. My gaze automatically turned towards him. A thousand queries ran through my mind in a fraction of a second with possible reasoning.

He drove, which means he wasn't much hurt.

A scream was about to escape my lips when I saw him gesture for me to keep quiet. I stifled that cry in my throat.

The next moment, he covered the car. He didn't want anyone to know about the accident. He seemed physically fine, but guilt was written all over his otherwise composed face.

"I'm fine. Do not ask me anything further. Let's go inside," is all he pleaded before pushing me inside the house and locking the door behind him. He went straight to bed without changing his clothes. He didn't want to eat.

"It's just a matter of a few hours before police will come. I want to fix things for you before I leave."

He stayed composed for some time before breaking down. I had never seen a man of his stature break down like this.

Between the laments, he was repeating, "I have killed a man! I have killed a man! I'm a murderer. Moreover, I flew from the site. I never peeked behind. He must have died on the spot. I was unnerved. I was scared for you and family. I'm ashamed of myself. Being a doctor I'm supposed to save lives. How can I take a life?

I tried to comfort him, "That was a moment. You may have taken an unfair decision. Your intentions were not wrong. Did you hurt him intentionally? For a second, he was calm when I asked him to recount what had happened. From the beginning, he narrated...

"As I left the hospital, I was completely tired and all I wanted was that familiar warmth of my home. I pressed the accelerator softly and my car zoomed along. I tried to play music on the FM radio but the transmission was interrupted due to the storm. Then I tried to find my pen drive. But let it go and rather focused on the road. Visibility was low, so, I was extra careful.

I noticed a person at a distance on an otherwise deserted road. He had a bar-like thing in his hand. He was trying to cross the road. I considered the need to press the brake but the speed wasn't much and he was at distance and could cross the road before my car could have reached him. I had kept my foot on the brake, so, had the need arise I could press it easily.

He almost crossed to the other side and I started shifting my foot from brake to accelerator when I noticed him stopped on the way and took about a turn, I panicked as the car had almost caught up with him and was about to hit him.

I pressed the brake hard, but the man was hit. The next moment he was in the air and with a loud thud fell over the windscreen before rolling down in front of the bonnet.

I was dumbfounded. All of this had happened in a moment. Right when I was so attentive and aware of the situation. Why on earth he stopped and turned at the last instant?

Besides me and the person lying in front of my car, no one else was in sight. It took me a fraction of a second. I reversed my car slightly, moved aside and fled the scene. I never looked behind and nor I tried to look in my rear-view mirror. This is SO not me dear."

He was crying. "I only pressed the brakes when I was in front of my house," he further said.

"So, you are not sure whether the man was hurt or died? You are just assuming it," I inquired.

"The impact was such that he must have died on the spot. I'm sure," said he.

We kept our fingers crossed and prayed for the person. Though I was scared as hell, I tried to be as calm and composed as I could- At least on the surface. I called a few friends and family members for advice. One of our acquaintances went to inspect the site and help the victim.

On the site of the accident, there were some scattered fragments of glass from our car's windscreen. Other than that, no injured person was there. Even no traces of blood were found on the site. We tried to find out if any case was registered or if someone was taken to the nearby hospital. But there weren't any.

The victim had disappeared in thin air. We kept a check for any such reported cases.

The guilt of being fled from the scene was so much that my husband was devasted. Both of us weren't able to sleep or eat for days.

My husband happened to handle a patient a few days later. Who has been assaulted with a metal bar? When that patient came to his senses, he narrated his story.

After listening to his story, we were immensely grateful that my husband fled from the site that day. Otherwise, he would have been in the same situation.

It was the same location. Around midnight, an accident occurred, and the driver stopped his car to check on the victim. The victim sprinted back to the upright position and hit the driver with the bar. Another person appeared out of nowhere. They robbed him of all of his belongings including the car and left him bleeding and helpless in the middle of the road. Without a phone and any money.

It was much later in the wee hours when someone spotted him and brought him to the hospital.

Later few more such cases were reported.

Whatever the situation, never stop your car in a deserted location. Better to surrender to the police if ever this kind of situation arises.

Be vigilant. Be safe.

CHAPTER FORTY-THREE

I See My Glass Half-Full

I read a story during my childhood. It had a great impact on my thought process and played a huge role in deciding what I wanted to be in my life. The story goes like this:

There were two brothers. One was a drunk who beat his family. The other one was a respected and successful businessman, loving and caring towards his family. People always wondered how two brothers from the same parents, brought up in the same environment, could be so different.

When asked, the first one replied, "I had become like this due to my childhood. I used to see my dad drunk and doing all the wrong things, so I ended up like this."

The second one also replied, "I had become like this due to my childhood. When I was a little boy, I used to see my dad drunk and doing all the wrong things, and I decided that this was not what I wanted to be."

It is not the situation that determines our life, but how we respond to it. The situation was the same for both brothers but their response was different.

If I wasn't treated well by some acquaintances, it shouldn't deter me from making things better for someone following in my footsteps.

If I wasn't treated well by my in-laws, it doesn't justify doing the same to the next generation. It's easy to react in the same way, but it takes inner strength to let go of things and make the future peaceful.

while we can't change the situation, we can always choose how we respond to it. As they say, two wrongs don't make a right, and an eye for an eye will eventually make the whole world blind.

It's up to you whether you see the glass as half-empty or half-full.

CHAPTER FORTY-FOUR

Let the Bitterness Go

Do you remember an incident when you exploded in an argument or witnessed someone exploding over something very insignificant?

We all must have witnessed or experienced it at some point in our lives.

When trivial issues are not addressed at the right time, they snowball over time into disappointment, bitterness, and hard feelings. When the accumulation of frustration crosses your threshold, you explode.

In most cases, there is an underlying feeling of being treated unfairly or wronged by another person. This feeling is normal to a certain extent, but once it becomes overwhelming, the person on the receiving end grows bitter, and resentment creeps in.

Learn to identify a toxic relationship and address it.

If you find yourself unable to let go of an issue or forgive someone, you are probably dealing with this issue. Negative thoughts can take over, and lingering negativity for a long period leads to bitterness.

You can address it yourself by gaining insight into it. Identify the cause and the individual responsible for it.

Once you identify it, you might be tempted to avoid it to protect your wellbeing. However, facing it is key to healing, and that path often leads through forgiveness. Find a way to make peace with your past and move on.

Letting go is not easy, but you can do it. Initially, lots of emotions like resistance, fear, and anger will arise. Process each feeling.

Self-compassion helps you heal. Try to see things from another perspective, as it fosters empathy and understanding. There is always a reason or explanation for certain behavior by another person. **Show empathy**.

Focus on the positive things. Among all the negative happening around you, there has to be something positive. Look for it. Remember when "Glass is half empty, it's always half-full." **Lean into gratitude.**

If you feel that someone is taking advantage of you, try stepping into their shoes. If you can't find a reason and justification for it, learn to say a confident '**NO**'. Doing it going out of the way and resenting later is going to harm both, you and your relationship.

If you are feeling put by a person repeatedly, having that person in your life is not a good sign. **Learn to recognize gaslighting.**

Do not keep unrealistic expectations. The ways of showing appreciation can differ but still hold equal values for two people.

Remember, finding a balance between acceptance and forgiveness is the key.